Social Conscience and Moral Responsibility

Teaching Ethics
Across the American Educational Experience

Dominic P. Scibilia, Editor

Social Conscience and Moral Responsibility

Teaching the Common Good in Secondary Education

Edited by Jane E. Bleasdale
and Julie A. Sullivan

Series edited by Dominic P. Scibilia

ROWMAN & LITTLEFIELD
Lanham • Boulder • New York • London

Published by Rowman & Littlefield
An imprint of The Rowman & Littlefield Publishing Group, Inc.
4501 Forbes Boulevard, Suite 200, Lanham, Maryland 20706
www.rowman.com

6 Tinworth Street, London SE11 5AL, United Kingdom

Copyright © 2020 by Jane E. Bleasdale and Dominic P. Scibilia

All rights reserved. No part of this book may be reproduced in any form or by any electronic or mechanical means, including information storage and retrieval systems, without written permission from the publisher, except by a reviewer who may quote passages in a review.

British Library Cataloguing in Publication Information Available

Library of Congress Cataloging-in-Publication Data Available

Library of Congress Control Number: 2020930404

ISBN 978-1-4758-4691-1 (cloth : alk. paper)
ISBN 978-1-4758-4692-8 (pbk. : alk. paper)
ISBN 978-1-4758-4693-5 (electronic)

Contents

The Series Preface   vii
Dominic P. Scibilia

Foreword   xi
Michael Duffy

Social Conscience and Social Responsibility: Working toward the Common Good in Secondary Education   1
Jane Bleasdale

1   Words on Writing   4
    Julie A. Sullivan
      Interlude by Jane Bleasdale   21

2   Our Values, Our Biases, and Our Actions: Can They Get Along?   22
    Nancy Johnson James
      Interlude by Jane Bleasdale   35

3   Humanistic Social-Emotional Learning   36
    Margaret Peterson
      Interlude by Jane Bleasdale   50

4   Teaching Digital Ethics   51
    Nicole M. Cuadro
      Interlude by Jane Bleasdale   59

5	Espousing Equity and Inclusion in an English Class: A Unit Plan for a Literature Class in Secondary Education *Austin Pidgeon*	61
	Interlude by Jane Bleasdale	75
6	Ethical Decision-Making from the Roman Catholic Tradition *Alex Porter Macmillan*	77
	Interlude by Jane Bleasdale	90
7	Critical Skills as the Foundations to Ethical U.S. History Lessons *Tricia Land*	92
	Interlude by Jane Bleasdale	106
8	Ethics in Mathematics Classroom Discussions *Robert C. Bonfiglio*	107
	Interlude by Jane Bleasdale	120
9	Health Care Ethics for Adolescents: Stirring Self and Social Awareness *Richard Marfuggi*	121
	Interlude by Jane Bleasdale	134

Epilogue 135
Dominic Scibilia, Series Editor

Editor and Author Biographies 136

The Series Preface
Dominic P. Scibilia, PhD

What is the American social compact on education? From Jefferson's vision of a public education that forms and informs a democratic citizenry to current education secretary Betsy DeVos's call to ease church-state regulations regarding education, proposing $5 billion of public money to fund private and religious education (as a means of providing fair access to better schools than implied substandard public schools), the current state of our national educational narrative is often framed by claims in conflict or claims that public education is deficient.

A great deal of the debate regarding the American educational experience since 1987 has focused on deficiencies—what students cannot do. Many works by commentators like Rudolf Flesch (1986), Allan Bloom (1987), and Erika Christakis (*The Atlantic* 2017) critically observe that students cannot read or write or are unable to distinguish right from wrong or that the trends in national public educational policy encourage a dystopian view of public schools.

In response to the conflicting claims about education in America, pedagogues propose whole curricula, design lessons, and implement assessments framed with SMART Goals, Backward Curriculum Design, Summative or Formative measurements of learning, and Professional Learning Communities as antidotes for what ails schools from kindergarten through graduate schools.

The past thirty years in American education feel like an extended autumn. The debaters and conversation partners look too often like people witnessing the sepia hues of the American public educational experience—as if it has been dying. Caught in the melancholy that sometimes accompanies autumn, catching us up in a deep appreciation for the beauty of the season and the advent of death, we miss the seeding that is occurring. Our children in public schools as much as in independent or religious schools are indeed learning to read, write, reason critically, create, and know right from wrong—imagine morally.

Insight into the state of our national educational narrative, the social compact we have with our children regarding their education and with each other regarding the forming and informing of democratic citizens, rises from the witness of the patriots who teach especially ethics.

Teaching Ethics across the American Educational Experience gives us pause to consider the moral seeding underway throughout American schools. Indeed, students are learning how to distinguish right from wrong, to engage reason, emotion, and imagination when acting as moral agents. During the spring of 2018, Tom Koerner, vice president/publisher for Rowman & Littlefield, encouraged me to raise the witnesses whose words and works provide evidence of effective learning, of the seeding of the moral imagination for future citizens.

MARCH 14, 2018

It has been a month since the shootings and killing of seventeen adults and students at Marjory Stoneman Douglas High School in Parkland, Florida. The front page of *The New York Times* frames the infancy narrative of the student social movement #NeverAgain. Like many student movements from around the world (from Colombia, Mexico City, and Taiwan to the call for public education in Valparaiso, Chile) Parkland High School students call for social change.

Broadcast news services witness the national growth of #NeverAgain as the Parkland students call for a national walkout from school at 10:00 a.m. today for a seventeen-minute memorial to those who died on February 14. Online and television cameras broadcast pictures of students and adults from Parkland, Atlanta, Decatur, Washington, D.C., New York City, and, as the Central and Mountain time zones reach 10:00 a.m., from Chicago, Littleton in Colorado, and schools in Idaho. They walk out from classes with and without administrative permission.

Adolescents soon to break in on adulthood express ideas like civic responsibility, social reform, political will, civil disobedience, constitutional rights in conflict, and legislative change. They announce their advent as voters. How did those young citizens arrive at moments of political engagement? What stirred their social and moral imaginations—seeing visions of a good society in contrast to their experiences of a flawed society? How did they cultivate abilities to assess critically the functions and dysfunctions within our American political systems?

Someone designed and implemented educational experiences that proved to be effective learning moments in social ethics. The evidence for effective learning in that student movement is not measured by a test score; rather, the evidence comes in the students' applications of their moral imaginations to social questions. Look at how they act, at what they do. As their moral imaginations provoke civic engagement, students become the sort of citizens that advocates for public education, from Jefferson to Dewey to Weingarten, hope would graduate from American schools.

MARCH 14, 2019

There are teachers from kindergarten through senior year of high school, from undergraduate classrooms to postgraduate professional seminars and corporate committees who design and implement ethics instruction and assess the effectiveness of learning ethics. Those teachers have been responding consistently since the late 1980s to the caustic criticism that a moral vacuum exists in American schools: That Johnny and Jane cannot tell right from wrong as well as read.

Teaching Ethics across the American Educational Experience celebrates the commitment of educators who teach ethics. The contributors in each of the five books in this series take time to write about how students are learning ethics—how instructors teach ethics. It is an unusual writing for teachers. Few preschool and K–12 teachers receive the time to reflect critically on and write about instruction, especially teaching ethics. The demand for scholarship in higher learning rarely considers works seated in a critical reflection on instructional design and implementation—practical works rather than the intellectual kind.

In *Teaching Ethics across the American Educational Experience*, teachers take the time to consider ethical instruction and its effectiveness. They present models for ethics instruction and learning from kindergarten through professional life. Lesson plans, integrative plans across a school's curriculum, templates for implementation and means of learning assessment populate five teacher-friendly, student-centered, practical monographs. The series' goals encourage teachers to pause and in that critical contemplative space consider integrating ethics into their American students' educational experiences.

These five texts call readers to respond to our witness—the instructional experiences that invite students to be citizens carrying out the American Experiment. *Teaching Ethics across the American Educational Experience* offers the witness of administrators, teachers, parents, the teachers of teachers, and students that will stir moral imaginations to design and implement learning ethics, to open effectively American hearts, souls, and minds. We raise a witness to the current state of our national educational social compact.

Brian Gatens, superintendent of The Emerson Public Schools District in New Jersey (Emerson, New Jersey), opens a literary space wherein administrators and teachers model integrating ethics instruction within a social-emotional learning framework—education attending to the whole child.

Kristen Hawley Turner (Drew University) convenes a community of educators from elementary school through graduate educational studies for dynamic conversations on the ethical dimensions of teaching digital literacy.

Jane Bleasdale and Julie Sullivan's (University of San Francisco) volume invites middle- and high-school teachers to offer models of teaching ethics (stirring self and social awareness that leads to civic agency) in public and independent high schools.

Daniel Wueste (Clemson University) gathers a symposium of university faculty (many of whom are members of The Society for Ethics across the Curriculum) proposing models for teaching ethics across undergraduate studies.

Philip Scibilia (Medical Humanist) calls together graduate school professionals who offer prescient instructional models for teaching narrative ethics within a Medical Humanist praxis across health care curricula.

Foreword

Michael Duffy, EdD

What is the purpose of education? Throughout history people have claimed many purposes for education: skills building, pleasure in learning about the arts or history, social status, job promotion, to name a few. The University of San Francisco (USF) is a Jesuit University. USF is one of twenty-seven throughout the United States and part of a network of Jesuit Universities around the world. The purpose of education in the Jesuit context is that of liberation and freedom. A key element of the pursuit of liberation and freedom is that of engaging the social reality. Combined, all of those dynamics contribute to the pursuit of creating a more just and humane society and world.

In much of the world today, the social reality is troubling. Looming catastrophic climate changes, mass migration, income inequality, rise of the political right, the rise of an empowered white supremacy, gun violence, sexism, homophobia, and attacks on minority groups are all impacting the consciousness of society and the global community. A feeling of hatred toward others, a lack of trust, and a general uncertainty about the future all seem palpable.

Education appears under attack as well. Over the past few decades, a diminishment of the value of education among some segments of society has been creeping into the social and political climate. Not everyone needs to attend college, higher education is too expensive and is more about indoctrination than learning, public school districts are losing funding, and Catholic schools are struggling with fundamentalist interpretations of Catholic identity. The messages being sent to the twenty-first-century adolescents paint a bleak picture.

Teaching Ethics across the American Educational Experience, and of particular interest *Social Conscience and Moral Responsibility—Teaching the Common Good in Secondary Education*, comes at a crucial moment in time. The approaches of each of the authors in this volume seem to weave a salve on the wounds of society. Let every voice be heard, bring those on the margins into the center, promote equality, understand your bias—the lesson plans and instructor materials speak to the challenges of society and offer some hope for the next generation.

The contributors each include elements of justice with a lean toward liberation and freedom in their designs for learning. Sullivan conveys how the power of writing well frees students and teachers from biases and frees them to hope and dream of equality. James invites readers into instructional strategies that assist teachers in exploring bias and approaching equity and justice. Peterson considers bias through the instructional lens of Humanistic Social-Emotional Learning.

Cuadro logs instructors into teaching digital ethics and asks students to consider the roles and responsibilities of being a digital citizen. Pidgeon explores identity, race, and ethnicity in the English classroom, examining critically one's self and social awareness. Macmillan offers the Catholic ethical imagination as a dialogue partner in the quest for common goods for students of all faiths or no faith at all. Land provides tools that strengthen students' skills in social moral inquiry, revealing bias and transforming the classroom into a culture of accountability. Bonfiglio presents mathematics as a reflection of the students in the classroom. Problems illuminate the realities of their lives, and mathematics as a language unlocks new ideas and hidden discoveries, all of which tell a deeper truth.

Marfuggi explores extra-curricular experiences wherein high school students demonstrate their ability to learn applied ethics—focusing on healthcare through inclusive dialogue.

The models for ethics instruction in *Social Conscience and Moral Responsibility: Teaching the Common Good in Secondary Education* resonate with the purpose of education leading to self and social liberation and freedom. The contributors raise a vital educational witness of a shared vision of the future that is more just and humane.

Social Conscience and Social Responsibility: Working toward the Common Good in Secondary Education

Jane Bleasdale

How we teach ethics has been an ambiguous instructional area for many years. In religious schools, it is left to the work of the religion teacher, and in public schools it is often incorporated into a civics course. Across private and public school curricula, there are multiple points where teachers can incorporate learning ethics, often in interdisciplinary ways.

Social Conscience and Moral Responsibility—Teaching the Common Good in Secondary Education focuses on how educators in high schools (grades nine to twelve) incorporate the teaching of ethics effectively across all disciplines. We have also included chapters on writing and the impact of journaling and reflection.

What is ethics? What do people believe is ethical? In this volume, contributors focus on ethics as *the common good. We believe central to the common good is the belief that the flourishing of one is bound to the flourishing of all. A school, university, or institution is strengthened when it creates the conditions for inclusive human flourishing* (Black and Brigham, 2018). When we understand that the common good can exist only if we embrace their interdependency and intradependency, our perspective on how we engage self and others changes.

To understand ethics, teachers and students have to question what it means to be ethical. Who gets to say what is right and wrong? For adolescents, this is a key stage of their development. They are on the journey of finding themselves, discovering the depth of evil the world holds and the incredible love *agape* that humans can and do express for each other on a daily basis.

Ethics is the understanding of the balance between good and evil, right and wrong, helping versus hurting. Adolescents discover ethics to be as simple as doing what lifts others up or puts them down or as complex as making life-and-death decisions—literally. Growing toward an understanding of right and wrong—of creating a community that believes in and upholds *the common good*—is the focus of our work in this text.

Each writer focuses on the teaching, learning, and practicing of ethics. We encourage readers to look at this from a lens of equity and inclusion to move from a *fairness lens* to *an equity and inclusion lens*. Each chapter gives an instructional witness that challenges racial, gender, and other oppressive stereotypes. We particularly want to emphasize an ethical pedagogy. Educators, we call on you to reflect on your classroom climate with great intention before you begin this work. In particular, consider the following questions:

How do you create community in your classroom?
How do you support students in speaking up?
How do you address power and privilege and the silencing of voices?
What practices do you use to call students out and invite students in?
How do you share your own vulnerability while also creating and respecting boundaries?

In chapter 1, "Words on Writing," Julie A. Sullivan invites readers into a collaborative instructional process in secondary education. The reflective process grounds instructional awareness in an ethics of equity, welcoming contributions from the diversity in voice and style one finds across any high school curriculum.

In chapter 2, "Our Values, Our Biases, and Our Actions: Can They Get Along?" Nancy Johnson James stirs critical instructor and student consciences into analyzing how personal and social biases can distort the expression of many of their highest human values.

Margaret Peterson writes convincingly about "Humanistic Social-Emotional Learning". In chapter 3, she calls readers to reflect on their implicit biases and actively monitor what they say and do in the classroom that might trigger or retraumatize students, disrupting their social moral development.

Nicole M. Cuadro, in chapter 4, "Teaching Digital Ethics," charges readers to move far beyond behavioral issues like netiquette and provides meaningful activities and reflections that support professional and personal growth in the field of digital ethics.

In chapter 5, "Espousing Equity and Inclusion in an English Class," Austin Pidgeon invites readers to try on strategies for literature teachers that create an equitable and inclusive curriculum. His instructional models afford students the opportunity to consider their individual and collective identities, focusing primarily on the role that race/ethnicity plays in identity development.

Alex Porter Macmillan, in chapter 6, "Ethical Decision-Making from the Roman Catholic Tradition," offers the chance to break free from a religious bias within public education about the place of the study of religion. He opens an opportunity to see Catholic moral teachings as a dialogue partner with students of all faiths or no faith at all.

In chapter 7, "Critical Skills as the Foundations to Ethical U.S. History Lessons," Tricia Land encourages readers to enter into a U.S. history course that provides teachers with the tools to strengthen learners' inquiry skills as a means to reveal bias. Tricia Land's instructional praxis transforms the classroom into a culture of accountability and responsibility in the pursuit of ethical U.S. history lessons.

In chapter 8, "Ethics in Mathematics Classroom Discussions," Robert C. Bonfiglio incorporates mathematical concepts and methods into discussions on ethics, providing insight into questions like *Whose truth matters?* and *How does problem solving translate to considering ethical debates?* The questions that frame Bonfiglio's instructional model surface biases and encourage concern for logical reasoning and the power of language leading to ethical understanding and the development of inclusive communities.

Richard Marfuggi in chapter 9, "Health Care: Ethics for Adolescents," tackles *the received wisdom that ethics is a discipline best undertaken at the undergraduate level and the tacit corollary that adolescents are unable to engage in meaningful dialogue on a subject that has little impact on their young lives no longer holds*. What follows is a discussion of high school students' ethical evolution through an extracurricular educational conference on leadership in medicine that celebrates student insights through inclusive dialogue.

REFERENCE

Black, Stephen K., and Erin M. Brigham (eds) (2018). *Catholic Identity in Context: Vision and Formation for the Common Good (The Lane Center Series)*, Vol. 6. San Francisco: University of San Francisco Press.

Chapter 1

Words on Writing

Julie A. Sullivan

This chapter provides a collaborative instructional process in secondary education, grounded in an ethics of equity that prepares students for writing in college and their future careers. The collaborative process under consideration welcomes diversity in voice, form, and style and relocates the task of teaching written, oral, and digital communication from one person or department to the whole educational community.

ON WRITING INSTRUCTION

Let's talk about writing—more specifically, all of that written work teachers assign to students. All instructors require students to write in some shape or form. They may put a lot of thought into those assignments, aim for multimodal approaches, plan steps for students to check in with teachers or review their progress with each other, and create assessment processes that seem fair and equitable. Instructors may also assign writing projects—because they're part of what's expected—and simply have a due date (or end time for the essay exam). Or teachers may fall somewhere in between.

Work with predominantly incoming college students informs the approach in this chapter—prompting concerns around what may help high school instructors prepare students for the increase in workload, and in particular the writing load, encountered in college courses (or on the job). Research into the transition to college and college-level writing from the student perspective reveals that many college students feel blindsided by the college workload, especially the amount of written work required.

In addition, writing is a tricky beast. So much about what *works* in writing is subjective and situational. The author needs to cater to a particular audience, in a particular context, for a particular occasion. Students aren't wrong when they say that every teacher wants something different, because each teacher may be looking at different aspects of writing, often the ones they favor or know how to do (or assess), and these likely differ from what another teacher in another class marks up or down. When asked what is *good* writing, the best answer may be *it depends*, and that can be maddening.

When teachers assign writing in classes, they think that students will rely on the knowledge they gained from previous classes and apply it in other courses. In reality, transfer from class to class (or across subject areas) is not as automatic or intuitive as one may expect (Wardle, 2007). Students may need help to see connections across all the work they do, so instructors may need to be more explicit around where and how concepts link. What seems obvious to educators may not be as clear to students.

To add to the challenge, the demand for writing ability continues to increase. Employers looking at college graduates often cite written and oral communication skills as among the most important for hiring and promotion (Hart Research Associates, 2018). So the foundation laid in high school helps establish habits and expectations not only for the work assigned in college but for the students' future careers.

No pressure.

Here's the good news: Teachers don't have to do this alone. While forming an approach for assigning, supporting, and assessing student writing may feel daunting at times, this can be a team effort established among colleagues at every school. With some organizing around the types of assignments offered, the language used to discuss shared core concepts and the grading practices used for assessment, writing transfer from class to class can be more successful and sustainable.

Many conversations are happening at the university-level around writing-enriched curriculum, writing transfer, equitable grading practices, and similar theoretical approaches. There may well be similar conversations at the high school level, but it's certainly not the norm. (Hint: it's not the norm at the college level either.) Writing across the Curriculum (WAC) has been a goal in higher education for more than forty years, and, to be honest, it's still a work in progress.

Even at schools where efforts to infuse writing-enhanced or writing-enriched curricula have been ongoing for decades, we still have instructors in some departments complaining that their students *can't write*—and not seeing it as their jobs to do something about that. Those of us charged with *teaching* writing wonder who could be better to highlight the writing conventions of a certain field than the person who teaches the content of that discipline.

Is it reasonable to expect the teacher who assigned the writing project to be the one to support students in developing that assignment—rather than rely on a teacher in another department or a tutor to do so? Of course, it is. Yet many of us still secretly hope that someone else will take care of the writing part—and that doesn't have to be the case. We can work together to support our students in their writing development.

In an effort to link writing across subject areas, many institutions of secondary and higher education are working toward interlinking or reflective curricula that weave writing into some aspect of every subject area. One example: I recently had the opportunity to be part of a faculty learning community (FLC), a collaborative working group, focusing on some of these exact issues.

Inspired by what was being done at other colleges and universities, and what the FLC learned through the literature, the collaborative brought together faculty from computer science, nursing, education, business and management, psychology, and rhetoric to discuss the projects assigned to students. The FLC quickly found that faculty were hungry to have these conversations—many had struggled to make the link between first-year writing courses and what the students did in the discipline courses (and if faculty were struggling, just imagine the leap being asked of the students).

What came out of the collaborative working group were the seeds of a shared approach to talking about written, oral, and digital communication projects—more specifically, participants created a glossary (a portion of which will be included in this chapter). It may seem small, but it's an important first step of many to be taken across the curriculum, and it's a start of an ongoing conversation. In addition, within the rhetoric department, a group of faculty have been exploring anti-racist grading practices. These are also a work in progress and part of an ongoing conversation.

This chapter serves as a sort of *how to* for having comparable conversations at your institution. There may be resistance. The ideas may push against what teachers think is a key part of one's job as a teacher. The challenges may become personal—it has certainly challenged me personally. But experience attests that having the conversation is worth it. Even more, it's essential for instructional practice and, most vitally, for students. Making collaborative conversations part of the teaching norm will be a catalyst moving educators and students toward our common goals.

A common goal throughout this text is to instill an ethical approach to teaching (and assessing) student writing as students encounter ethics instruction across the curriculum—a *walking-the-walk* approach. The instructional process involves facing personal demons and challenging preconceived notions around what makes *good* writing. It should also involve collaboration between colleagues to develop a unified approach that supports each other's efforts. This approach involves embracing humility, recognizing that each teacher can keep learning new ways of thinking about the work that we do.

RECOGNIZING BIAS, FACING DEMONS, AND UNLEARNING THE FIVE-PARAGRAPH ESSAY

The first order of business in building an ethical approach to writing instruction is to recognize what teachers bring to the table. Putting aside what instructors think they are supposed to teach or even what they think writing instruction should include, start by thinking about what appeals to readers. What grabs readers' attention? What convinces them in an argument? What evidence seems valid? What credibility does the writer have to establish for the reader to give their ideas weight? What formats tend to be utilized in particular fields? Is there common terminology or specific practices for using or citing sources?

Teachers also need to confront the demons from the past around their own writing experiences. Perhaps teachers are concerned about teaching writing because some stodgy instructor told them that their writing was below par. Even though others may have said otherwise, maybe even praised or raved about something one wrote, some part of one's psyche may give more weight to the negative comments from that stodgy instructor. Perhaps a teacher even fears that she may become that instructor for her students, so it's easier not to engage too deeply in discussions around writing.

Teachers also need to embrace the idea that—and this could hurt a bit to admit—instructors have writing preferences but don't always know how or if one is allowed to encourage these forms of writing from students. All educators work under various external (institutional) guidelines, requirements, restrictions, and constraints that may severely limit diversity in writing.

In the process of embracing an ethical approach to teaching different forms and formats, instructors should raise challenges to the concept of Standard English, or even Standard Academic English, because those standards reflect the tendency by the dominant culture to suppress diverse voices and rarely is something students and instructors actually *want* to read. At the same time, the number of contexts in which so-called Standard Academic English is utilized continues to dwindle—with academic journals and audiences broadening their interest in reading a variety of types of texts.

Recently, the concept of recognizing different forms of *languaging* has been offered as an alternative to Standard Academic English. Although coined by Merrill Swain in the mid-1980s (Swain, 1985: 98), languaging relates to the cognitive process of "making meaning and shaping knowledge and experience through language" and resonates with efforts to debunk myths surrounding standard forms of English by recognizing identities and diversity within languages.

Languaging opens the opportunity for students to apply their funds of knowledge (Moll et al., 2005) gained through personal, cultural, social, and academic experiences to their messaging. It also extends to all forms of communication, linking many methods of connecting to an audience and encouraging the use of whichever medium (or combination of mediums) may best engage that particular audience—further supporting different literacies and multimodal approaches in education.

Part of the myth of Standard Academic English is the idea that there should always be three reasons for each argument—in other words, the perpetuation of the five-paragraph essay format. Even though this format is a state-mandated requirement in some areas, the first challenge many first-time college students encounter is that most professors expect more than five paragraphs for their essays. This shift in expectation also throws off the students' time management abilities, as they got quite good at anticipating the time needed to pump out five paragraphs.

The reality is that most forms of writing are not presented in five paragraphs. Consider where we do see the five-paragraph format; it's almost exclusively in academic writing contexts—meaning writing assigned for a class. That format does not appear anywhere else, really, not even in academic journals. The reason we still have that format may well be that it's easy to teach, easy to read quickly, and perhaps even easier to assess quickly. There's no fault being laid here. Who could blame any teacher with a classroom full of students for wanting to assign what can be read and graded efficiently?

Educators should consider whether sticking to that format is serving the students or instructors well, and whether creating assignments that reflect real-world (academic, civic, or professional) contexts may be more engaging for writers and readers alike. For example, one student recently relayed her research about the economic crisis and effect on the people of Venezuela in a song, complete with facts and statistics related to the issue. Her performance was met with resounding applause from her classmates, who felt entertained as well as informed.

Given student reaction, should a teacher penalize that student for not having a perfect PowerPoint presentation? In reflection on that classroom experience, I gave her feedback around her paragraph construction and integration of information, yet I did not argue with her choice of medium or ability to connect her topic with her audience. Will she always be able to convey her research in song? Maybe not, but in this situation, it was possible and the autonomy to read the situation and make the appropriate rhetorical choice will, hopefully, stay with her.

SOME QUESTIONS TO CONSIDER

- What do I appreciate in the writing that I read—how is this reflected in what I expect from students? What forms/formats are useful or interesting or likely to be seen again by students?

- Do I have any demons around my writing? Or questions around my ability (or desire) to teach writing—what's fueling that?
- Do I have others to collaborate with to support efforts in this area?

ADDRESSING RESISTANCE

One of the biggest obstacles to achieving the goal of supporting writing across all disciplines is fear. Sometimes this fear manifests as resistance (*It's not my job to teach writing.*), as a concern around ability (*But I don't know how I write, I just do it. How can I teach it?*), or lack of time (*I don't have time to teach writing on top of all the content I have to cover.*). Yet teachers continue to assign writing-based projects in nearly every subject area on a regular basis—as it should be—and, even more importantly, students will continue to encounter a demand for writing skills in the future, in nearly any career they could pursue (DeVoss et al., 2013; National Writing Project and Nagin, 2006).

These obstacles can be mitigated through forming systems of support and a writing-enriched curriculum approach in all subject areas. This is especially helpful to offset the fear of doing it wrong—of not feeling confident in one's abilities to teach or grade writing—and the tendency to grade based on what can be quantified, such as the number of grammar errors. It is a common experience for teachers to tell students that so many errors would be an *A*, and this many errors would be a *B*, and so on. But this is far from what instructors value as good writing when they read it.

Not only are grammar rules fluid (and constantly evolving—just look at the Oxford/serial comma debate), but this approach puts little consideration or weight on how the so-called error affects the piece of writing as a whole. Does the piece make its point clearly? Is the evidence provided valid and convincing? Is the analysis or explanation logical? As a result, students learn that *revising* means to change the grammar issues. This doesn't teach the students much about how to improve or develop their ideas in writing or other forms of communication.

To offset the potential fears and possibility of resistance among teachers, acknowledge that those concerns or attitudes may exist and open the opportunity to work together to find options that may work for the teaching community. Recognize time is limited, so find methods for working and learning together, in face-to-face meetings or through online mechanisms that keep the conversation going. In addition, establishing a common language can help create bridges among teachers working in different content areas (more on this to come).

SOME QUESTIONS TO CONSIDER

- What fears or concerns are making members of the educational team resistant to a writing-enriched curriculum approach?
- How can participants acknowledge those concerns and create space for moving forward anyway?
- What methods of communication are available for keeping the conversation going?

WRITING FOR TRANSFER: AN ETHICAL APPROACH TO TEACHING AND SUPPORTING WRITING

Because each discipline or subject area has its own set of conventions, the best support for students is reinforcing similar concepts as cornerstones for clear, well-developed writing that transfer from one discipline to the next. While working in a certain subject area, instructors can also point out aspects within the written work that are conventions of that particular field or genre, similar to how a film may have aspects that make it clearly a horror movie versus a romantic comedy.

Noting similarities and differences—while reinforcing some chosen core concepts—will help students bridge the skills they've developed from one area to another area, supporting their writing across contexts. Even though it seems like it should happen naturally, research shows that the majority of students do not transfer skills without explicit connections being made (Yancey, Taczak, and Robertson, 2014).

Each subject area or field of study has certain *threshold concepts* (Land, Meyer, and Smith, 2008). They define ways of thinking in a discipline. Imagine them as a gateway that students pass through in understanding—what was once incomprehensible becomes clear and can be applied to what one is working on. These concepts are shared by others in the same discipline or discourse community and create space for people to think and collaborate in their work, because they share this common understanding.

Although each subject area or discipline has their own set of threshold concepts, some concepts can extend across disciplines. Scholars in writing and composition studies have identified as many as thirty-seven such concepts in just this area of study (Adler-Kassner and Wardle, 2015), for example, the concept that writing involves making ethical choices.

How does an instructor surface threshold concepts in a high school classroom without adding a ton of work? Consider which core concepts will be foundational and/or immediately transferable to another course. It may help if a teaching staff can agree on common core concepts across all classes and subject areas. Teaching for transfer can also promote engagement—however, there is some debate around the *false contexts* of writing in a classroom.

Students need to be rhetorically aware of the context in which they are writing and how it may connect to/reflect other contexts (Bacon, 2000). When writing in a false context—for the teacher—students may not recognize how skills can transfer. When writing for a real world context (where there's exigency or purpose), they are more likely to see how skills they've used in one project can connect to future ones. For example, having an assignment where students pretend to write a letter to an authority figure versus having to send that letter to that authority figure. For the student, this may feel more purposeful and motivate them to up their game in the process.

CORE CONCEPTS AND GENRE CONVENTIONS

Here are a few concepts that could be applied across contexts:

- *Rhetorical Situation:* this one is key because it can include many essential sub-concepts:
  o the *Writer* (or rhetor),
  o the *Audience* (an individual/group who can receive the message and take action—whom they're writing to shifts with context and medium),
  o the *Context* (the different occasions, events, and spaces for writing),
  o the *Purpose* (reason for writing—to inform, instruct, persuade, entertain),
  o the *Genre* (type of writing/field of writing and the formats and different conventions/practices in different fields or subject areas),
  o the *Exigency* (relevance/urgency),
  o the *Stance* (attitude/tone/positioning), and
  o the *Medium* (design/benefits/limitations);
- *Voice:* the writer's and those from sources included in the project (via research or interviews)—perhaps highlighting the strengths in their unique points of view;
- *Thesis/Main Idea/Claim:* statement of main point(s) (including a sense of how the point will be explored or proven);
- *Structure/Organization:* the format of the *content* and how it meets the assignment requirements;
- *Knowledge:* what it is, how it's formed and shared (how they already have so much and can use what they know to link to what they are learning);
- *Metacognition:* creating awareness of our thinking, writing, revising processes (this is being practiced as early as in elementary school under current curriculum, but this concept is not always pointed out to students);

- *Critical Thinking:* this pairs with metacognition because one involves the other, but making thinking critically explicit, providing steps or hints, can be enlightening—even just reminding students to consider the five Ws (who, what, where, when, and why) can deepen their consideration of a text (their own or someone else's);
- *Peer Review:* not only a concept but a potential practice to incorporate into the student writing process (see more on this later).

These terms are just a starting point. Many of these terms appear in a glossary created by the previously mentioned FLC, but making such a list isn't unique to any one school. In fact, the FLC borrowed the idea from Dr. Kathleen Jernquist, who created a Common Rhetorical Language to unite writing instruction among STEM faculty at the U.S. Coast Guard Academy. Having a conversation around the core concepts and shared elements provides a backbone for writing instruction across the various classes and departments.

BEING TRANSPARENT ABOUT PROCESS AND FORMAT

According to Tinberg (2017), *Teaching for Transfer* in writing consists of (1) a set of organizing and foundational key terms and (2) a sequence of writing assignments, both informal and formal, that assist students in understanding and deploying those terms. He encourages his students to define the key terms and look for relationships among them, both in their work and in the work of others. Students can also add to the class list of terms as they encounter elements they feel are essential to writing or class discussions.

Transparency about the ways of organizing in your genre or field is critical. Note what formats are most common, if the format can be built upon (like adding points to a five-paragraph essay) or if it will appear in other contexts, possibly under different names (a summary/response essay becoming a marketing report). Call attention to common structures, such as forms of argument (e.g., definition, proposal, or cause/effect).

Expose students to different genres in the course of discussions on particular topics—for example, TED Talks, podcasts, academic journal articles, and articles from popular magazines. These encounters with diverse genres provide examples for framing conversations around genre and medium, while supporting efforts to develop multimodal approaches.

Because even the strongest writers need reminders on how to structure and organize their ideas, some teachers have adopted mnemonic devices to support students at the paragraph level. A couple of easy-to-remember ones are

- PIE (Point, Illustrate, Explain),
- TEA (Topic, Evidence, Analysis).

The two devices serve the same purpose of reminding the writer to start with a topic sentence and to not just share their ideas and thoughts but to incorporate insight from reading, research, or interviews along with their explanation or analysis. Tell students that their paragraphs may look more like PIIEIE and that some points may extend into another paragraph with additional evidence or analysis. The key is to have some flexibility so the structure can be adapted to different contexts, as needed.

SUPPORTING WRITING THROUGHOUT THE WRITING PROCESS

How can teachers better support student writers in their writing process? While some instructors are regularly in the trenches, working side by side as students develop and polish their ideas, many instructors (perhaps too many) assign a piece of writing, set a due date, and that's it. They may make themselves available during writing time in class or before/after school, but what percentage of students seek out that support and which type of students tend to seek that support?

As welcoming and approachable as instructors think they may be, students see a giant chasm between where they are and where teachers sit. Faculty members may have forgotten about this chasm, so picture walking up to a famous author or celebrity chef and asking a question. Do you worry about sounding like an idiot? So do students when approaching a teacher for support. Teachers can make efforts to bridge this chasm and better support their students by building check-in opportunities into the writing process.

One method is via peer review—still scary but something everyone has to participate in, and at least peers are in the same position of feeling vulnerable and potentially stupid. There are many methods for peer review. The one key factor for success is providing clear guidelines and support. Students need to understand what to read for (what aspects of writing or the assignment to focus on), how to provide feedback, and what to do with the feedback they receive.

The following are some options for giving students a sense of what to read for:

- Create a checklist (the instructor can create a list of requirements to hand out or create a list in conjunction with the students—on the board or in a Google document).
- Provide a rubric (with the areas of focus for this assignment clearly delineated).

To give students a sense of how to give feedback, building an environment of mutual respect is vital. Students can be given permission to disagree with each other but not to disrespect anyone (or their ideas)—everyone is learning and developing. To foster this approach, teachers can consider a recommended practice found in creative writing workshops to performance reviews in business alike, which doubles as an effective way to give feedback in general: provide the positive feedback first and then move on to the questions and recommendations.

Even though some may say this approach is just a form of sugarcoating the negative comments or even *burying the lead*, providing equal emphasis on strengths along with areas for further development is proven to offset the deficit model of education. The Eugene Muscat Scholars program at the University of San Francisco even uses a *StrengthsBuilder* tool in their bridge program for first-generation college students. Not only is it important to know what one is good at, so students can capitalize on their strengths, but it's also important to know what *not* to edit out of a draft.

What this *positive forward* approach may look like in a sample writing workshop environment:

1. Students are paired or put into small groups (no more than five to six people).
2. Students share drafts of their essays/projects (in class or online via a learning management system like Canvas or Blackboard).
3. Students are given time to read each other's drafts (if possible, this should be given as homework so there's ample time for reading, reflection, and writing out feedback).
4. Students should write out feedback, collecting all positive comments in one section of their document and questions, ideas, or recommendations in a separate section.

My classes use a model acquired from Barbara Ohrstrom, a former instructor at the University of San Francisco. The model asks students to organize their comments into four sections:

- *Reflect*: An overall reflection of the main ideas in the text they read (or, what Peter Elbow calls, the "movie in their mind" as they read).
- *Praise:* Listing the elements that stood out as effective for the context of the assignment—the more specific, the better.
- *Recommendations for Improvement:* Listing the moments in the text where questions arose or improvements can be made, with specific ideas or suggestions for how to improve or further develop.
- *Wrap-Up:* A brief summing up of the state of the text (with an encouraging "you can do this" endnote).

When the groups meet, the students go around the circle sharing only the *Reflect* comments first—to compare what each reader perceived as the main points or ideas. This immediate feedback tells the writer whether their overall message, main claim, or purpose is clear. Then the students go around the circle again to share their areas of *Praise* for comparison. Next, the students go around to share their specific *Recommendations for Improvement*. Finally, the students share their *Wrap-ups* with positive endnotes. This format works as long as students are specific, respectful, and supportive of each other in their comments.

Some college instructors benefit from smaller class sizes and flexibility in their use of class time. Because the context is higher learning, a college instructor does not have to have all of the students in the same room for the entire class, so they can meet with only a portion of the class in a particular class period, while the others are working elsewhere.

High schools may offer some flexibility, as well, where students can report to the library, work outside the classroom or in the hallway, or work with a student teacher. If not, peer review can be done in a full class or small group format within the classroom, and with clear guidelines and the instructor moving around the groups for support, it can be successful. Don't fear the trial and error involved in finding a format that works. The workshopping done in well-structured/well-supported peer review is often the part of the class that students find most valuable at the end of the semester.

In a different peer review model, instructors can assess the type of feedback students are giving each other, sometimes without even reading the drafts. Sounds crazy, but multiple instructors at multiple schools are focusing on the ability to give and receive feedback, and to create a plan for revision, rather than the drafts themselves. They're still teaching writing elements and meeting with students who would like additional support, and some are still reading drafts at some point in the writing process but the idea is to concentrate on the skills that are most transferable.

One system for this approach is found in *Eli Review*—a set of tools for creating a feedback-centric learning environment. Teachers employ these tools to create spaces where students provide feedback anonymously on classmates' texts. An instructor can read every comment and coach students around improving the feedback given. Based on insights from peers, which improve with practice (and instructor support), students develop a plan for revising, editing, and proofreading. Students can learn to *re-see* their work and remember to fine-tune their texts for final submission.

Another method is through the more traditional method of requiring drafts or conferences with the instructor. Drafts can be daunting because they are more to read. The upside is that final drafts tend to be stronger, cleaner, and quicker to assess. Having set conference times will offset the lack of showing up for after school tutoring sessions. Teachers have to find what works best for their students, their assignments, and their sanity.

Overall, we're aiming to model ethical approaches to supporting the students' voices and ideas. As you talk about ethics and infuse ethical teachings into your subject area, you can demonstrate an ethical stance by honoring their efforts to learn through their writing practice and develop their critical thinking and writing skills in the process.

SOME QUESTIONS TO CONSIDER

- Are there particular concepts or genre conventions that would advance student writing skills if students already understood them or put them into practice?
- Are there aspects or building blocks of those concepts in the work students present that teachers can highlight for them to capitalize on or continue developing?
- What is the writing process a teacher should expect from students—what does a teacher do to scaffold or support that process? Is there a way to make at least some of the assignments have a real-world audience?
- What resources or spaces can be utilized to support students' efforts?

ETHICAL GRADING AND ASSESSMENT

Assessing student work and assigning grades gets into treacherous territory. It would be a mistake if the conversation on the myths of Standard Academic English were not followed with a consideration of the accompanying effects of dominant culture in assessment.

Assessment of writing is often subjective. It can *feel* like an A or B more than a teacher can actually quantify what makes one essay an A versus a B. Rubrics can help make quantifying easier. Even involving students in rubric development or grading scale development can make the process feel more fair and equitable—but is it? Or are educators still expecting a fish to climb a tree (to cite a quote often attributed to Albert Einstein though it may stem from an *educational allegory* published in a journal of education dating back to 1898).

Recent work in anti-racist writing assessment practices call upon us to consider our approaches to assessment and whether teachers are perpetuating harm done by dominant cultural hegemony in the process of providing students feedback and assigning grades. This may sound intimidating, but it's an important way of promoting social justice and equity in classrooms. Inoue (2015) wrote in the introduction to his book on this subject:

> If we are to enact helpful, educative, and fair writing assessments with our students, given the history of whiteness and all dominant academic discourses promoted in schools and disciplines, we must understand our writing assessments as anti-racist projects, which means they are ecological projects, ones about sustainability and fairness, about anti-racist practices and effects.

A key part of this practice is the language instructors use in writing assessment—what one says in the feedback—as well as the criteria a teacher uses in grading, and how those criteria are weighted. Grading by grammar alone does not cut it.

By looking for ways to assess fairly the work of diverse student populations (rather than trying to push all student writing through the same filter—a filter that may not even reflect the future contexts for writing), and by designing and implementing writing assessments that are socially just, teachers can work to support the efforts and honor the experiences of all students. An equity ethic transgresses the standards of the educational system that favors students from literacy-rich environments by recognizing the value of diverse languaging experiences.

Racism isn't the only aspect of hegemony that can affect assessments of student writing. Consider how other aspects of intersectional identity formation can enhance classroom writing and grading practice. Perhaps a teacher favors work done by female writers, or unintentionally rewards arguments that reflect particular political affiliations, missing an opportunity to support a transgender individual in exploring their unique perspective on a particular issue of community interest.

On our campus, a small team has been exploring anti-racist grading agreements. Following the lead of colleague and mentor Dr. Nicole Gonzales-Howell, the team has been building upon the work done by Inoue (2015), Elbow (with Danielewicz) (2008), and faculty from San Francisco State University and the University of California–Davis in adopting a grading approach that rewards process, behaviors, engagement, and effort. Because not all students arrive at college with the same educational opportunity or experiences, but all have experiences to share, the contracts being adopted reward what a student brings to the process (not what a learner lacks based on rules set to favor literacy-privileged populations).

This switch in grading approach has been met with some pushback by students and faculty who, conditioned by a system where grades are a currency linked to scholarship money, fear the unfamiliar. Some instructors question the rigor involved; others wonder what their job is if it isn't to judge student product. But these contracts challenging social-educational privilege are rigorous and there are plenty of requirements to fulfill. The team holds the bar high for quality and do not penalize students for taking a risk or making mistakes along the way.

As long as a student completes the assignment *in the spirit and manner asked* (Inoue, 2015), meaning the student met the requirements, made a genuine effort to apply workshop feedback, and turned in all assignments on time, they will receive a *B* in the course. To achieve an *A*, a student needs to engage further with the content, the class, or the community.

The engaged student may take a variety of additional actions, such as visit the campus Writing or Speaking Centers, exchange drafts with a classmate for proofreading, deepen research into the essay topic, attend a guest speaker on campus, or share an article related to a recent class discussion—the list has a dozen items. A teacher's response should be *Yes* when students suggest other ideas or options. Again, further engagement is the key—and likely, this engagement will advance their written, oral, or digital communication skills in the process.

There's a bit more to it, and each member of the team has their own version of the grading agreement—none of which are identical to Inoue's or even between colleagues. For instance, I have changed the contract every semester since inception as I learn more about what best serves the students at my institution. The team has had multiple conversations about what's working and not working in grading contracts, and what adaptations could be made to Inoue's model, to consider inclusivity and Universal Design approaches.

Although students sometimes enter the class skeptical of the grading, most find the grading approach to be fair and, in some cases, even inspiring. In a reflection, one recent student wrote:

> When initially joining the class I asked myself whether or not the default grade of a B was a fair assessment. After going through all of the assignments I would say yes the B default grade is a wise choice made by professors. It mutually shows that as long as work is handed in with guidelines followed you will pass the class no problem. As stressful as college is this helped my mental health a lot and made me understand what it means to be a writer. We don't write to fulfill an assignment. We write to understand and show the world what we have learned, and how it pertains to the population. I hope this grading contract stays within the curriculum.

This reconsideration of grading and assessment processes may also raise some of the demons from each teacher's own writing experiences. While it may be tempting to adopt the *I experienced this and I turned out fine* approach, one exposes the long-term effects of how the traditional assessment of learning doesn't serve all students equally.

In the discussion about writing in all classes across the departments of the school, instructors need to consider the effects their feedback have on the students—and the effects that grades have on the students' options for the future. No one is suggesting teachers should let students *slide*. Teachers can be both rigorous and socially just in instructional practice.

SOME QUESTIONS TO CONSIDER

- What is my current approach to grading and providing feedback to my students?
- What kind of written, oral, or digital work do I tend to favor? Why?
- What policies exist at my school that speak to grading or assessment? Where/how can I challenge those approaches or make (even small) changes toward being more ethical and just in my practice?

PUBLIC SPEAKING AND DIGITAL FORMATS

In this day and age, writing or composition cannot be divorced from other forms of rhetoric. Educators probably never should have thought of writing and speaking as separate, because they share so much in their creation and development, even if the final forms may differ. For example, in public speaking courses, students are likely to see that five-paragraph format. They may even use it for most of what they present. This can be frustrating for those teachers looking to toss this format out a third-story window but the reality is that the format is still useful in this context. So it stays.

Similarly, thinking about how to write for public speaking events can help writers when they move their text to an online context. Writing for digital formats tends to involve shorter sentences in a more conversational tone than the typical academic essay. In reality, many teachers require students not only to write but also to present in their classes, yet offer little-to-no support around presentation preparation or public speaking skill development. Students are just supposed to figure it out.

Many universities, my own included, are moving toward holistic approaches to teaching rhetoric (a.k.a. *the Full Rhetoric*) using multimodal approaches and multimedia projects. The goal is to encourage students to use the media they are likely to encounter in their future communications and careers in a setting where all can learn and develop.

Having a unified approach to teaching writing can include an approach to teaching public speaking, digital communication, and presentation formats. The important thing is to consider how these communication formats can link and find opportunities to be explicit about the connections between writing, speaking, and producing.

SOME FINAL QUESTIONS TO CONSIDER

- In what ways do I support students' efforts not only to write but also to speak or produce digital texts or presentations?
- Are there places within existing lesson plans where I can make links to oral or digital communication more explicit?
- Are there resources available at my school or in my community to support these efforts?

ENCOURAGEMENT

Throughout the different chapters of this text, each contributor aims to be explicit in the connections between writing, speaking, and producing. They use some key core concepts and point out how these ideas can be applied in different contexts. All efforts are in service of creating schools that welcome a diversity of voices—especially those often excluded.

But this is only a starting point. In your school, with your colleagues, you may be able to create a process that works for you. If you teach English, be careful not to take on the whole task yourself. If you teach some other subject, look for ways to support these efforts and infuse your practice with a written, oral, and digital communication approach that links to your discipline. And as you find approaches that work, share them! (Others will be looking for ideas and appreciate your experience and insight.)

A key part of this process is removing the idea of teaching writing from the shadows—or the underbelly—of education and to take the onus of teaching written, oral, and digital communication off of one person or department. We all require it, so we should all do our part in providing the richest experiences and support available. This is an evolving process that we can continue to improve if we work together—for our own benefit and that of our students.

REFERENCES

Adler-Kassner, L., and Wardle, E. (2015). *Naming What We Know: Threshold Concepts of Writing Studies*. Logan: Utah State University Press.

Bacon, N. (2000). "Building a Swan's Nest for Instruction in Rhetoric." *College Composition and Communication*, 51(4), pp. 589–609.

DeVoss, D. N., National Writing Project, Hicks, T., and Eidman-Aadahl, E. (2013). *Because Digital Writing Matters: Improving Student Writing in Online and Multimedia Environments*. San Francisco, CA: Jossey-Bass.

Elbow, P. (with Danielewicz, J.) (2008). "A Unilateral Grading Contract to Improve Learning and Teaching [co-written with Jane Danielewicz]." *College

Composition and Communication, 3. Retrieved from https://scholarworks.umass.edu/eng_faculty_pubs/3.

Hart Research Associates (2018). "Fulfilling the American Dream: Liberal Education and the Future of Work." Retrieved from https://www.aacu.org/research/2018-future-of-work.

Inoue, A. (2015). *Antiracist Writing Assessment Ecologies: Teaching and Assessing for a Socially Justice Future*. Fort Collins, CO: Parlor. Retrieved from https://www.academia.edu/14213706/Antiracist_Writing_Assessment_Ecologies_Teaching_and_Assessing_for_a_Socially_Justice_Future.

Land, R., Meyer, J., and Smith, J. (2008). *Threshold Concepts within the Disciplines*. Rotterdam: Sense Publishers.

Moll, L. C., Amanti, C., Neff, D., and Gonzalez, N. E. (2005). "Funds of Knowledge for Teaching: Using a Qualitative Approach to Connect Homes and Classrooms." In *Funds of Knowledge: Theorizing Practices in Households, Communities, and Classrooms* (pp. 71–88). Lawrence Erlbaum Associates. https://doi.org/10.4324/9781410613462.

National Writing Project and Nagin, C. (2006). *Because Writing Matters: Improving Student Writing in Our Schools*. San Francisco, CA: Jossey-Bass.

Swain, M. (1985). "Communicative Competence: Some Roles of Comprehensible Input and Comprehensible Output in Its Development." In S. Gass and C. G. Madden (eds.), *Input in Second Language Acquisition* (pp. 235–253). Rowley, MA: Newbury House.

Tinberg, H. (2017), "Teaching for Transfer: A Passport for Writing in New Contexts." *Peer Review*, 19 (1), pp. 17–20.

Wardle, E. (2007). "Understanding Transfer from FYC: Preliminary Results of a Longitudinal Study." *WPA Journal*, 31 (1/2) pp. 65–85 (Fall/Winter).

Yancey, K. B., Taczak, K., and Robertson, L. (2014). *Writing across Contexts: Transfer, Composition, and Cultures of Writing*. Logan: Utah State University Press.

INTERLUDE BY JANE BLEASDALE

We begin with a chapter on writing because, as educators, we have all experienced the push and pull of *writing across the curriculum*. The premise of this book is that the teaching of ethics and promotion of the common good are the responsibilities of all educators, as it is with writing. Learning, processing our own understanding, and then sharing via the written word is essential for a student to develop their own voice. Julie Sullivan's experience at various levels of education is utilized daily in the classroom where she teaches writing to college freshmen. As a colleague, I have seen firsthand the incredible impact this work has on students, some of whom are considering their own biases for the first time.

The work in this chapter sets the stage for chapter 2, "Our Values, Our Biases, and Our Actions," by Nancy Johnson James—an accomplished educator and fierce advocate for empowering students often most marginalized by our schools.

Chapter 2

Our Values, Our Biases, and Our Actions: Can They Get Along?

Nancy Johnson James

The lessons in this chapter were written with an agenda. Each lesson and activity determines the extent that the personal values of teachers and students are actively engaged in actions, reactions, and choices. The hope is that teachers and students explore how personal and social biases can distort the expression of many of the highest human values. Students and teachers will participate in deep and challenging thinking about whose humanity we honor and whose we ignore.

The goals of this chapter are the following:

- clarifying and articulating community and personal values;
- understanding the role that bias (conscious, unconscious, implicit, and explicit) plays in society and personal relationships;
- recognizing how biases against people who are different can lead us to behave in a way that is contrary to those values,
- shifting thinking so the students and teachers challenge their own biases and begin to make their values the first criteria upon which they think and act,
- understanding that to achieve real social changes requires employing our highest values beyond the people and community with whom we feel comfortable and even beyond the people and communities we like or agree with; and
- engaging in action toward social justice/the common good based on those community and personal values.

INTRODUCTION

One of the challenging aspects of teaching ethics is the expectation that the teacher will be a perfect role model at all times. That's not very helpful (or realistic). What is helpful is for teachers to approach the task by establishing some foundational understandings that will make the deep, challenging work possible. One such understanding is that diversity is valued as a benefit to society.

School communities vary from place to place. Regardless of the makeup of a particular student population, teachers should find ways to bring diverse voices into the classroom. There are a variety of online and print resources available that can expose students to a variety of perspectives. Those should be used but can't replace the impact of inviting guests into the classroom to engage in face-to-face conversation with students.

Another way that teachers can value diversity is to establish the practice of talking about people who are not in the room as if they are in the room. In other words, do not use any language or images in a person's absence that one would not use in their presence. In the United States, such considerations have been reduced to continual and unproductive arguments regarding *political correctness* and free speech.

Educators can lead an effort to speak, think, and behave in ways that consciously seek to avoid dominating and doing harm to others. In this way, teachers and students can also avoid causing harm and shame to themselves. The study of ethics is an opportunity to learn how to engage in inquiry in a way that is civil in addition to being critical, courageous, and caring.

Teachers are encouraged to refer to the Universal Design for Learning framework as they plan to use these lessons. Making sure that the lessons are accessible to all of the students one might encounter is a crucial part of strengthening the community. Give students the freedom to write (at least first drafts) in the language most comfortable to them. Allow students to represent their ideas in multiple ways (words, pictures, metaphor) and support students in using the most effective processing journal for them. This means there are no extra points for the kind of technology that students use, as long as they use what they choose effectively.

Make sure students have access to read aloud assistive technology. If a video is shown, be sure to select closed captioning and check with students to make sure the volume is at a comfortable level. Allow students to move closer or further from the screen according to their needs. Because students may need to move around the classroom, consider how well the pathways accommodate movement for different kinds of bodies. Finally, make accessibility a natural part of the learning environment by building as many supports into the lesson as possible.

The lessons and activities in this chapter are ones in which students document their thinking in creative ways. While the activities lean heavily on visual arts, teachers and students are encouraged to bring other arts forms into the process.

The first lesson uses the art of collage-making to generate student thinking with regard to how they view and value others. They can also begin to question the accuracy of their own judgments.

The second lesson begins with a mapping strategy to support students in defining bias. Students are then called upon to engage in discourse about their definitions in small groups and ultimately arrive at a definition for the classroom.

The third lesson is one in which students reflect on how they are viewed in society and how that has impacted them.

The fourth lesson contains multiple activities that may need to be stretched out over several sessions. It is one in which values are studied and then classroom values are established.

The fifth lesson uses journalism to take the class outside of the school building and into the world. Students will be encouraged to think about how we decide who is and is not of value. By seeking issues in their local community, students can begin to think about how they would like to respond to an issue based on established personal and classroom values. Opportunities to take action toward justice or the common good should be encouraged for students as individuals and as a classroom community.

In the sixth and final lesson, students will return to the use of personal stories to consider how to make future choices.

How can we know that students are reaching the intended goals in this chapter? Where should educators look for the evidence of learning? Students should be able to

- define bias, both implicit and explicit, and provide real-world examples by referring to current or historical events, and/or data relating to systematic examples of bias in society;
- explain why and how bias functions in opposition to their values or how it may serve their values;
- articulate their personal values and how those values are employed as they face situations every day;
- seek, listen to, understand, and empathize with people from diverse backgrounds and perspectives. This requires students to pursue information from sources with whom they are not familiar and may disagree and to document those sources;
- use their values to shift how bias may be present in their own perspectives. This employment of their values should be documented in their process journals, group discussions, and/or group work;
- use their values to reflect on past experiences in order to influence how they may respond in the future. Again, this reflection should be documented in their process journals, group discussions, and/or group work;
- use their values to work collaboratively to identify a situation in which bias is or has led to unfair treatment and to develop a plan to take action in opposition to that bias. Students should identify an issue of bias that they care deeply about and want to change or influence in some way;
- think compassionately with regard to people who have differing and even opposing viewpoints and work to develop responses that honor their values

and help others to grow. Students should show an understanding of multiple viewpoints in their documentation. They should be able to listen to and ask questions of people with differing viewpoints;
- employ their values to challenge bias in their own thoughts, words, and actions, and in others; and
- articulate (assertively if necessary) well-constructed opinions and positions.

USING A PROCESS JOURNAL

Students and teachers[1] are encouraged to use a process journal as they move through these lessons. Because the lessons will undoubtedly touch upon sensitive and challenging subject matter, one role of the process journal will be to provide a place to work through thoughts and ideas that may be difficult to express. It can also be a place where students ask difficult questions. Teachers should review and respond to process journals but also maintain student confidentiality.

Teachers and students can interact with their journals in ways that make sense to their personal thought processes. Handwriting, sketches, doodles, pictures, articles, and poetry may be kept in the journal. If the process journal is used for assessment, teachers are encouraged to work with students to develop a rubric upon which to base that assessment. One strategy to employ is to begin with journal assignments based on a very basic rubric and then to later develop a student-driven one that reflects the values of the class.

Additional lesson activities can include having students pull language from their journals in order to write poetic responses to the concepts covered in the lessons. Teachers can choose whether or not to focus on using a specific poetic form. Classes can go into their local community and use photography to document bias and/or actions that heal the harm. Teachers should invite students to draw on their personal interests, skills, and talents. Using the journal in this way helps students to synthesize all of the content of the lessons.

SAMPLE PROMPTS

Ongoing (Useful for Any Topic/Class Period)

What do I understand better today?
How did I come to this new understanding?
Why is this new understanding important?

Topic Specific (e.g., Acting on Our Values)

What is the issue?
Why do we think this is a problem?

Who is being harmed?
How are they being harmed?
Who is causing the harm? What are they doing?
What role does bias play in this issue?
How can we respond in a way that helps to heal the harm?

ASSESSING STUDENT WORK AND/OR SELF AND PEER ASSESSMENTS

Teachers are encouraged to use the Unit Outcomes to help guide the assessment of student work. As students engage in the activities and process their thinking in the journals, do they show an understanding of the points clarified in the Unit Outcomes? Share the Unit Outcomes with the students in the beginning so that they can think about how the activities guide them to think about each point.

With regard to art-making, use the content of the art they produce to determine how close they are to understanding the Unit Outcomes. When engaging in assessment of the art itself, it is suggested that teachers utilize the *studio habits of mind*. These also provide a foundation for self and peer assessments. The studio habits of mind clarify ways in which artists think and work in order to produce art.

THE STUDIO HABITS OF MIND

Develop Craft—This habit has to do with developing technical skills.
Engage and Persist—Embracing problems and maintaining focus.
Envision—Mentally picturing what can't be seen and imagining next steps.
Express—Conveying meanings, feelings, and ideas.
Observe—Engaging the senses more closely than ordinary seeing or hearing.
Reflect—Thinking and talking with others about work and learning to judge one's own work.
Stretch and Explore—Learning to explore new areas, be engaged without a plan, and reaching beyond perceived capacity.
Understand Art Worlds—Interacting as an artist with other artists.

SUGGESTED RESOURCES

Arts Integration: Project Zero, http://www.pz.harvard.edu/search/resources
Religion and Spirituality: Patheos, www.patheos.com/teachers

Restorative Justice: RJOY, Restorative Justice for Oakland Youth, https://restorative justiceontherise.org/resources/restorative-justice-for-oakland-youth-rjoy/

Race and Media: Colorlines Magazine, www.colorlines.com

Assessment: Studio Habits of Mind, https://www.acoe.org/site/default.aspx?PageType=3&DomainID=71&ModuleInstanceID=485&ViewID=6446EE88-D30C-497E-9316-3F8874B3E108&RenderLoc=0&FlexDataID=281&PageID=137

Unit 1 Title: Defining Bias

Topic 1: Defining bias: What do we mean when we talk about bias?

Lesson Learning Outcomes
Students will

- define the word "bias";
- examine how bias functions in society;
- explore how bias functions in the lives of individuals;
- learn to use a journal to document thinking and research;
- engage in academic discourse.

Potential Journal Prompts
Ongoing
What do I understand better today?
How did I come to this new understanding?
Why is this new understanding important?

Bias
Describe a time when you experienced bias? Was it directed toward you or someone you know?
How did you or that person respond to the bias?
How did you feel?
What response might have helped?

Activity 1: Warm Up
1. Students open journals to a blank page.
2. Write the word "bias" in the middle of the page. Students should use black ink.
3. Give students three to five minutes to write every word that comes to mind when they hear the word "bias." Students should use blue ink (or some other color).
4. Students should then use a third color ink to connect words on the page that seem to go together.
5. Write one sentence to describe what bias is.

Activity 2: Draft Definitions in Small Groups
1. Each student shares their sentence defining bias.
2. Students work together to write a definition of bias.
3. Students write the definition out on large or poster paper.

(Continued)

Activity 3: Display and Discuss
1. Post the small group definitions of bias around the room.
2. Students should read each definition and put any thoughts or questions that come to mind in their journals.
3. Students can also use sticky notes (or some other method) to ask questions or make comments about each definition.
4. Using the small group definitions, and facilitation by the teacher, students can now develop and agree on a definition of bias for the class.

Activity 4: Read about Bias or Experiences of Bias (Suggestions)
1. Teaching Tolerance Article: https://www.tolerance.org/professional-development/test-yourself-for-hidden-bias
2. Where All Bodies Are Exquisite: https://www.nytimes.com/2017/08/09/opinion/where-all-bodies-are-exquisite.html
3. "Stranger in the Village" from *Notes of a Native Son* by James Baldwin
4. Read some dictionary definitions of bias

Activity 5: Assess Our Definition
1. How did we do? Have the readings changed our thinking? Should we make any changes?
2. Final agreement on class definition.
3. All students should write that definition in their journal.
4. Teachers are encouraged to keep a process journal alongside students.

Unit 2 Title: Our Community Values

Topic: Beliefs and Values

Unit Learning Outcomes
- Understand bias and how it impacts the lives of people.
- Understand how bias can affect our ability to make ethical choices.
- Recognize that everyone has biases that can affect their decision-making.
- Recognize that the relationship between bias and power impacts the lives of some people/groups in more harmful ways than other people/groups.
- Recognize how we can learn to align our choices with our values and to question our own biases and behavior.

Lesson Learning Outcomes
Students will
- identify the unifying themes in the core beliefs of most major religions/belief systems and how these kinds of basic beliefs are the foundations of individual and societal values;
- study and compare the core values of belief systems to help them articulate their own values;
- create deeper awareness and understanding of the beliefs that guide people.

Potential Journal Prompts

Ongoing

What do I understand better today?
How did I come to this new understanding?
Why is this new understanding important?

Values

What do I believe?
Where did my values come from?
How are my values evident in my words and actions?

Activity 1: Belief Jigsaw in Teams

1. Students will choose three to five religious/spiritual traditions (e.g., Judaism, Buddhism, Islam, Ifa, Hinduism, or Christianity).
2. Students identify a statement of core beliefs from that religion or philosophy (e.g., The Ten Commandments, the Five Precepts of Buddhism, or The Four Agreements).
3. Students create a list of the beliefs and then cut them into strips. Each piece of paper should have one statement. Make sure the statements are written in contemporary language.
4. Divide students into teams. Each team should get full sheets of paper with the name of a religious tradition written at the top. Each team should also get a set of the statements of beliefs. The statements should be mixed up.
5. Challenge the teams to see which group can match the statements with the religious tradition correctly and first.

Activity 2: Discuss the Belief Statements

Students should stay in teams to discuss the belief statements they sorted. They should respond to guiding questions, such as

- What were the similarities in belief statement from these religious traditions?
- What were the differences?
- How might they be helpful?
- How might they be harmful?

Activity 3: Recommend Classroom Core Values

While still in teams, students will now agree on three statements of values to recommend to the classroom community. Each team will put their values on a poster with a one- or two-sentence explanation of why they feel it is one the class should adopt.

Activity 4: Vote on Class Values

1. All of the team values should be posted.
2. Each student will receive five stickers. They must then review all of the team values and put a sticker next to the five they think the class should adopt.
3. After they vote, the class tallies the votes and then agrees on how they will display the class values.

Unit 3 Title: How Bias Behaves

Topic: Implicit Bias

Unit Learning Outcomes
Students will

- understand bias and how it impacts the lives of people;
- understand how bias can affect our ability to make ethical choices;
- recognize that everyone has biases that can affect their decision-making;
- recognize that the relationship between bias and power impacts the lives of some people/groups in more harmful ways than other people/groups; and
- recognize how we can learn to align our choices with our values and to question our own biases and behavior.

Lesson Learning Outcomes
Students will

- think about how the implicit bias others might hold may impact their lives;
- practice engaging in civil discourse with others around challenging issues;
- practice showing empathy for peers.

Potential Journal Prompts
Ongoing
What do I understand better today?
How did I come to this new understanding?
Why is this new understanding important?

Implicit Bias
Activity
Students will respond to the following prompts in writing:

1. List three words or phrases that describe how people see you.
2. List three words or phrases that explain how you see yourself.
3. List three words or phrases that describe how you would like to be seen.

Organize students into groups of three for a small-group discussion using the following prompts. Starting with the first speaker:[2]

1. Describe a time when you or someone you know was either harmed or benefited in a situation because of bias (five minutes).
2. The other two people ask questions about the situation (two minutes).
3. The first speaker responds to the questions (three minutes).
4. The group should then envision how they would like to behave if put in a similar situation (five minutes).
5. Rotate to the next person and start the process again.

Assessment
Mini-Play/Skit
Each group will select one of the stories that were told and create a mini-play/skit (three to five minutes). They will then perform it for the class.

Assessing the Skit
Criteria to Consider

- Did the student(s) participate in the process?
  o At what level did the student(s) participate?
- Did the skit/story show an understanding of how bias looks in day-to-day interactions?
- Did the skit/story show an understanding of the impact of bias on individuals?

Unit 4 Title: Our Values, Our Biases, and Our Actions: Can They Get Along?

Topic: The Impact of Biases on Our Values

Unit Learning Outcomes
Students will

- understand bias and how it impacts the lives of people;
- understand how bias can affect our ability to make ethical choices;
- recognize that everyone has biases that can affect their decision-making;
- recognize that the relationship between bias and power impacts the lives of some people/groups in more harmful ways than other people/groups; and
- recognize how we can learn to align our choices with our values and to question our own biases and behavior.

Lesson Learning Outcomes
Students will

- explore and challenge their own understanding of the world around them and their judgments;
- become conscious of how implicit bias influences how we perceive people and situations.

Journal Prompts
Ongoing
What do I understand better today?
How did I come to this new understanding?
Why is this new understanding important?

Activity
1. Students will select a word written or printed on a notecard at random.
2. Each student will use pictures of people they select from magazines to create a collage that defines the word they received.

Word List: intelligent, friendly, safe, brave, beautiful, strange, dangerous, trustworthy, innocent, suspicious, efficient, strong, weak, uneducated, poor, clean

Assessment
Gallery Walk
Students display collages around the room and respond to each collage by commenting on sticky notes.

Guiding Questions:
Do the pictures chosen represent the word to you?
What would you add?
What, if anything, would you remove?
What are the similarities/differences in the pictures used?
Who is missing?

Discussion:
Can we know if a person possesses any of these qualities based on their appearance?

Unit 5 Title: Making New Neighbors

Topic: Bias and Community

Unit Learning Outcomes
Students will

- understand bias and how it impacts the lives of people;
- understand how bias can affect our ability to make ethical choices;
- recognize that everyone has biases the can affect their decision-making;
- recognize that the relationship between bias and power impacts the lives of some people/groups in more harmful ways than other people/groups; and
- recognize how we can learn to align our choices with our values and to question our own biases and behavior.

Lesson Learning Outcomes
Students will

- understand how bias functions on a societal level;
- think critically about how society expresses its values through the treatment of differing groups of people;
- learn to critique the sources of information they encounter;
- increase their awareness of current events, particularly in communities that are different from their own;
- learn to seek out multiple news sources in order to obtain information.

Journal Prompts
Ongoing
What do I understand better today?
How did I come to this new understanding?
Why is this new understanding important?
Bias and Community

Activity

1. Give each student or pairs of students a local newspaper. They should then go through the paper and highlight what they think are the most important stories of the day.
2. In pairs, students should choose a crucial issue from their highlighted stories and talk about why they think it is important.
3. Students should be asked to pay close attention to the kind of language used in headlines and articles, the photographs and captions, and the placement of articles and photographs on the page.
4. Students will then choose one issue (e.g., drug addiction or climate change) and seek out new sources online to explore how same/similar issues manifest in communities that are different from their own.

Questions to ask:

- How does bias affect how stories are told? How do we know what is true?
- How does the way the stories are told influence the community or society's response?
- How does societal bias infiltrate our ability to live up to our highest values?

Assessment
Rewrite the Story
Each student will have an opportunity to rewrite the news. The students will use their research to write a news article on the topic/issue they chose.
Assessing the Stories
Criteria
Refer back to the Unit Outcomes

- Does the student's story meet the overall Unit Outcomes?

Unit 6 Title: The Power of Stories

Topic: Our Stories

Unit Learning Outcomes
Students will

- understand bias and how it impacts the lives of people;
- understand how bias can affect our ability to make ethical choices;
- recognize that everyone has biases the can affect their decision-making;
- recognize that the relationship between bias and power impacts the lives of some people/groups in more harmful ways than other people/groups; and
- recognize how we can learn to align our choices with our values and to question our own biases and behavior.

Lesson Learning Outcomes
Students will

- explore and challenge their own understanding of the world around them and their judgments;
- become conscious of how implicit bias influences how we perceive people and situations.

Journal Prompts
Ongoing
What do I understand better today?
How did I come to this new understanding?
Why is this new understanding important?

Activity: Telling Stories
It's been said that "The shortest distance between two people is a story."
Process Journal Activity

1. Use journals for a three- to five-minute free-write about the following prompt: write about a time when a stranger behaved or spoke in a way that was different from what you expected when you first saw them. A time when you were pleasantly surprised by a stranger who was different from you.
2. Direct students to go back and read what they wrote.
3. Give students five minutes to edit their story while paying close attention to communicating the emotions they felt during the experience.

(Continued)

4. Get students into small groups.
5. Each student can be invited to share their story.
6. The small groups now have some options: (A) They can either select one story to expand on by adding new details, events, or characters. (B) They can find a way to combine stories to create a new story to share with the class. (C) They can co-write a completely new story.
7. Compile the stories so that they can be read by the entire class.
8. Have students respond in their Process Journals:
    - Which story resonated with you?
    - Have you had similar experiences?
    - Did any of these stories challenge your thinking with regard to a particular person or group?

CONCLUSION

The activities in this chapter may be challenging for students and teachers. They may lead to some discomfort and many questions. Hopefully they will also be inspiring and provide the foundation for new ways to think about living with integrity. Please remember that as students engage the topic of bias, they are participating in a conversation that most adults avoid because of its implications in their own lives. For that reason, students and teachers can expect mistakes, misunderstandings, and even conflict. Working through the tough parts takes courage, creativity, and faith in the ability of young people to make a difference.

SUGGESTED READINGS

Duckworth, Eleanor, ed. *"Tell Me More": Listening to Learners Explain*, New York: Teachers College Press, 2001.
Hetland, Lois, Sheridan, Kimberly M., Veenema, Shirley, and Winner, Ellen. *Studio Thinking 2: The Real Benefits of Visual Arts Education*, Second Edition. New York: Teachers College Press, 2013.
hooks, bell. *Teaching Community: A Pedagogy of Hope*, New York: Routledge, 2003.
Marshall, Julia. (2005) "Connecting Art, Learning, and Creativity: A Case for Curriculum Integration," *Studies in Art Education*, 46:3, 227–241, DOI: 10.1080/00393541.2005.11650076.
Perkins, David. *Making Learning Whole: How Seven Principles of Teaching Can Transform Education*, San Francisco, CA: Jossey-Bass, 2009.
Ritchart, Ron, Church, Mark, and Morrison, Karin. *Making Thinking Visible: How to Promote Engagement, Understanding, and Independence for All Learners*, San Francisco, CA: Jossey-Bass, 2011.

INTERLUDE BY JANE BLEASDALE

Understanding our biases and the impact they have on learning and instruction is a relatively new concept for many educators. In this chapter, Nancy James showed how essential it is for educators to challenge bias and values in the classroom. Her truly authentic process of using multiple modalities and engaging all students is foundational to this work. I encourage you as a reader to also engage in the process with the students—processing your biases before you engage others. As a student in my classroom, Nancy both challenged and inspired me to do better to be better—especially with the task of decentering whiteness.

Even though the second chapter exemplifies the next step in ethical education, Margaret Peterson's instructional design in Chapter 3 attends to the wider educational context of biases and values—the student's social-emotional life.

NOTES

1. Teachers are encouraged to keep their own process journal and to check-in with students periodically as they see an opportunity to integrate ideas or compare/contrast insights and experiences.
2. The other two people in the group should listen without interrupting.

Chapter 3

Humanistic Social-Emotional Learning

Margaret Peterson

This chapter offers a new model of Humanistic Social-Emotional Learning (HSEL) that starts with teachers looking in the mirror, reflecting on their implicit bias, and actively monitoring what they say and do in the classroom that might trigger or retraumatize students.

UNIT TITLE: HUMANISTIC SOCIAL-EMOTIONAL LEARNING

Social-Emotional Learning (SEL) has become increasingly relevant in education as researchers, policymakers, educators, and community and business leaders recognize the importance of preparing students to be successful in our culturally diverse global society.[1] SEL curriculum and lessons address the social and emotional needs of students, as well as the academic content. In an effectively implemented culturally relevant SEL curriculum, the students feel connected to one another, supported by each other, motivated to think critically with compassion, and able/prepared to make responsible decisions based on ethical principles.

Educators hope to contribute to a world made up of principled, compassionate people who seek to listen and understand one another, engage in open dialogue, and treat each other with mutual respect. At the same time, teachers live in a racialized society that has harmed students of color through structural violence. Race is a social construct designed to keep those with power in power and perpetuate white dominant culture. The traditional model for SEL puts the onus on students, most of whom live with trauma on a daily basis, to self-monitor and self-correct behaviors that are a result of systemic discrimination and oppression.

HSEL starts with teachers looking in the mirror, reflecting on their implicit bias, and actively monitoring what they say and do in the classroom that might trigger or retraumatize students. When a student has a behavior that is characterized by dominant culture as defiant, instead of reacting in a hostile way or confronting the student, de-escalation is more likely if the teacher remains collected, looks at what is happening at that moment in the classroom, expresses empathy, and talks calmly with the student.

Teachers must pay attention to who students are, the assets they bring with them to school, and the stress and trauma they live with on a daily basis. Within the United States, youth from historically marginalized communities are likely to experience structural violence in the form of poverty, unemployment, underfunded schools, incarceration, lack of adequate health care, poor housing, and much more. Instructional practices that target these students for tracking or placement in special education are a failure to respond to student needs.

Students experience discrimination when they are placed in low-level classes, when peers from the dominant culture self-select groups that exclude them, and when teachers have lower expectations or do not value their home culture. English Learner's (EL) identities often intersect with other historically marginalized students, such as those who are also immigrants, refugees, or have undocumented status. Even the label of EL can have negative consequences such as *othering* and result in long-term harmful effects both academically and socioemotionally (Rodriguez, Hussain, and Padilla, 2018).

School discipline policies such as zero tolerance, disproportionate suspensions, and criminalization of young men and women of color have a negative effect on the social-emotional health and well-being of students and contribute to lower self-esteem, lower self-efficacy, and a lack of agency (Ginwright, 2016).

Not only must instructors be constantly vigilant about one's own implicit bias and microaggressions, teachers must create an environment of mutual respect and validation in the classroom. Even when a student does not show visible signs of trauma, teachers do not know the physical, emotional, and lived experiences they carry with them into different spaces. For example, teachers may not realize that they hold deficit assumptions about students such as an expectation of defiance or lack of ability. Yet these teachers unconsciously retraumatize students when they do not challenge their students academically or when they react harshly to outbursts by students.

Invisible trauma is present more often than we suspect. In the 2016 Obama administration report on school discipline, Oakland Unified School District was highlighted for shifting the "paradigm of punishment and exclusion in response to real or perceived student misconduct." The report goes on to say, "These gains reflect deep structural changes at both the district and school site level resulting from more positive, restorative, and trauma-informed responses to student behavior, and a commitment to equity and inclusion" (16).

First and foremost, instructors must get to know their students and establish trust by being predictable and reliable. They should value and validate students' home cultures. If students speak another language, they should be able to do so in class. They should be celebrated for the bilingual and bicultural assets they bring to the classroom community. Teachers should have high expectations for all students. Students who feel connected to teachers and their peers perform better academically and have positive social-emotional outcomes (Suárez-Orozco, Rhodes, and Milburn, 2009; Tong, 2014).

The Center for Wellness and Achievement in Education (CWAE) founded the Quiet Time (QT) program in San Francisco Bay Area schools. QT has been widely implemented for over a decade in urban West Coast school districts and has demonstrated improved social-emotional competencies in students including, but not limited to, stress management, emotional coping skills, resilience, and self-actualization (Nidich et al., 2009; Orme-Johnson and Barnes, 2014; Wendt et al., 2015). In the QT program students are trained in Transcendental Meditation and meditate twice daily within the school day.

According to Roeser and Peck (2009: 120), meditation programs in schools foster "personal growth and social transformation through the cultivation of conscious awareness and volition in an ethical-relational context." *Social-Emotional Intelligence*, developed by CWAE, is a course for high school students designed to heighten and support self-awareness, personal responsibility, emotion regulation, growth mind-set, empathy, and responsible decision-making. This course has been recognized by the University of California as a college-preparatory elective.

The following ten lessons are adapted from the CWAE *Social-Emotional Intelligence* course. They can be used as stand-alone lessons or incorporated into any content area. It is recommended that students learn to meditate prior to beginning the lesson sequence and to dedicate the first fifteen minutes of each class or block to meditation. For information on meditation training, contact *CWAE*.

In addition, each of these lessons aims to shift the mind-set of how teachers are empowering students to take pride in and ownership of their lives to consider the following lens: *Is white dominant culture being perpetuated by placing blame on students who have been harmed by systemic oppression and/or experienced trauma? Are we asking them to change their behaviors so they conform to white-accepted values and norms?*

Lesson 1: Community Building and Trust

Topic: Students will use Restorative Practices (RP) to cocreate a classroom community by defining their values, developing agreements to make the class a respectful learning community, and creating a trusting environment by showing mutual respect for each other.

Lesson Learning Outcomes
Students will
- get to know each other's names and pronouns;
- build community agreements to create a respectful learning community;
- articulate the importance of an anti-racist, anti-judgment zone for the class;
- use RP to hold community circles with classmates.

Materials: Markers, tablecloth and centerpiece, paper folded into thirds for name tags.

Class Setup/Preparation: Move tables and chairs to make space for tablecloth in center of the circle, set up center of circle, put out paper and markers, and write agenda on board.

Activities:
I. Once all students have been taught Transcendental Meditation (or some other form of meditation or mindfulness), devote the first fifteen minutes of each class to meditation or mindfulness. Ring a bell; students meditate for twelve minutes. Ring a bell; students rest with eyes closed for three minutes.

II. Frame the Purpose of the Class
We seek to empower internal self-healing and resilience in students through building a community of support and self-reflective practice so students can enact transformative change on their external environment (i.e., working from the inside out). We will use restorative circles, participate in trust building activities, adhere to our cocreated community agreements, and meditate.

III. Introductions
(1) Who are we? Name tag + gender pronouns + draw two things that represent you on your name tag (e.g., hobbies, food, and sports teams).
   (A) What are pronouns and why do we use them? (Before class, read this article by the Human Rights Campaign Foundation, "Talking about Pronouns in the Workplace.")
   Pronouns are how you would like to be referred to when someone is talking to or about you. Our class is a respectful learning community for everyone, and to make sure that is always the case, we ask everyone to state their pronouns so we do not assume someone's gender identity. Pronouns are said when we introduce ourselves each meeting so that we can be introduced or reminded of someone's pronouns and to see if anyone's pronouns have changed since gender can be fluid. We ask everyone to refrain from using "Male" or "Female" pronouns to describe their pronouns since gender is not binary (def: the idea that male or female are the only two gender identities) and static. We try to specify with a combination of: he, him, his/ she, her, hers/ they, them, theirs, ze . . . only to name a few. If you are not sure of someone's pronouns, just refer to them by their name, use a gender neutral pronoun like (they, them, their), or ask them.
   (B) Provide time for making name tags.
(2) Ask for a volunteer to start the introductions. When done they should choose a direction and the next person will introduce themselves.
(3) Repeat names until everyone knows each other's names.

(Continued)

IV. Community Agreements

Ask students to reflect on what they need from their classmates to feel supported and to be able to share openly. Students write their contributions on a large Post-it (one idea per Post-it).
 (A) Students post their stickies on the wall and arrange them by similar categories.
 (B) Make sure to include an anti-racist, anti-judgment rule as a non-negotiable agreement. Unpack and discuss this deep topic as needed. Refer to the National Equity Project website for ideas and resources. Make sure all voices are heard. This topic should be revisited in each lesson until students are able to notice and call out implicit bias and microaggressions as they come up.
 (C) Assist students to define categories and then combine similar agreements. Have students discuss and decide which agreements will make up the Community Agreements for the class.

V. Closing Activity

Give one word about how they are feeling to be in this class with these classmates. Teacher volunteers to start the closing activity. Pick a direction for the circle.

Assessment: Exit ticket—What is one action you will do from now on as a result of what you learned about what your classmates need to feel respected in this space?

Lesson 2: Emotional Intelligence

Topic: Students will understand the difference between emotional intelligence (EQ) and intelligence quotient (IQ) and become aware of their strengths and learning styles.

Lesson Learning Outcomes
Students will

- understand the difference between emotional intelligence (EQ) and intelligence quotient (IQ);
- take a self-assessment of their EQ;
- articulate their strengths and areas for growth.

Reading: Emotional Intelligence: Why It Can Matter More than IQ (Goleman, 2005)
Materials: Chromebooks, tablets, or other devices for students to take online EQ test.
Class Setup/Preparation: Move tables and chairs to make space for tablecloth in the center of the circle, set up center of circle, write agenda on board, and display community agreements.

Activities:

 I. Ring a bell; students meditate for twelve minutes. Ring a bell; students rest with eyes closed for three minutes.
 II. Open the community circle. Check in with talking piece.
 III. Ask students what they know about EQ and how it is different than IQ. Elicit examples from the class. *Critical self-awareness* is the ability to be aware of one's actions, thoughts, and emotions and understand the impact those actions, thoughts, and emotions have on oneself and others.
 IV. Show the first 7 minutes 30 seconds of the YouTube video Emotional Intelligence—Why your EQ is more important than your IQ?
 V. Post Goleman's Four Pillars of Emotional Intelligence on the walls spread apart.

VI. Have students take the free online Global Emotional Intelligence Test. Then have students stand near what they feel is their strongest EQ based on their EQ score. Hand students the clip (from the aforementioned Goleman Four Pillars handout) that matches the pillar they are near. Students read the clip, and then give examples of specific actions they do that align with that EQ. For example, if a student's highest EQ score is self-management, they might say, "Whenever I don't do well on a test, I don't let myself get depressed. I say to myself: 'I will study harder, work with friends who understand the material better, and I WILL do better on the next test.'"

VII. Close the Circle—Students return to the circle. Students share in one word or phrase something that surprised them about their own EQ today. If nothing surprised them, what do they want to learn more about in terms of *critical self-awareness*?

Assessment—Students write a journal entry about something they might do differently now that they know their EQ strengths.

Lesson 3: Growth mindset

Topic: Students will understand the difference between growth mindset and fixed mindset and learn to cultivate a growth mindset to help them improve areas of their lives.

Lesson Learning Outcomes
Students will

- understand the difference between growth mindset and fixed mindset;
- ask self-reflecting questions to inspire their growth mindset;
- decide on one or two areas for growth they will pursue and monitor.

Reading: *Biology of Belief* (Lipton, 2005)
Materials: Student journals.
Class Setup/Preparation: Move tables and chairs to make space for tablecloth in the center of the circle, set up the center of circle, write the agenda on board, and display community agreements.

Activities

I. Ring a bell; students meditate for twelve minutes. Ring a bell; students rest with eyes closed for three minutes.

II. Open the community circle. Check in with talking piece.

III. Ask students if they know what a growth mindset is. Elicit examples from the class.

IV. Show the Power of Belief—Mindset and Success

V. Post the words EXPERT (*I can do this in my sleep!*) and NOVICE (*I have never done that!*) on opposite sides of the room. Tell the students to listen to the skills you will read and to move to the side of the room that they feel best matches their ability in that skill. After the teacher reads each skill, students move to their comfort level for the skill names. Pause between each skill to allow students to talk with each other by answering the following questions: EXPERT—What made you an expert? How did you get here? Were you born with this talent or did you have to work at it? NOVICE—What do you think it would take for you to move from novice closer to expert in this skill? What support would you need from others? What would you need to do yourself?

(Continued)

VI. Skills to read slowly with pauses for student movement and conversations: Cooking, using public transportation to get across town, playing an instrument, taking care of a sibling, playing a sport, riding a skateboard, translating for parents or relatives.
VII. Students return to the circle and in their journal make two lists: (1) things they already do/perform well and (2) things they do not feel competent in yet and would like to learn. Students circle their top choices from each list.
VIII. Closing Activity

In the circle, students share what they are good at and what they would like to improve. Other students call out if they can support their classmates in the areas they would like to improve. Each student must write down at least one person to support. Each student must find at least one person to support them in their efforts to improve. Students should exchange cell phone numbers and regularly check in with their partners to offer support.

Assessment—Students write a short journal entry about their chosen area of improvement and what steps they will take each day or week to achieve that area of growth.

Lesson 4: Emotion Regulation

Topic: Students will understand that everyone experiences a wide range of emotions, both positive and negative, and the ability to observe, describe, and express painful emotions without disrupting relationships or harming oneself is a skill that can be learned.

Lesson Learning Outcomes
Students will

- recognize healthy and unhealthy ways of reacting to stress.
- understand the connection between triggers, thoughts, feelings, behaviors, and physical reactions in the body.
- understand *thinking distortions* and how to recognize them in the moment.
- learn what the zones of emotion regulation are and ways to return to the green zone.

Materials: Student journals; sticky notes.

Class Setup/Preparation: Move tables and chairs to make space for tablecloth in the center of the circle, set up center of circle, write agenda on board, and display community agreements.

Activities:

I. Ring a bell; students meditate for twelve minutes. Ring a bell; students rest with eyes closed for three minutes.
II. Open the community circle. Check in with talking piece.
III. Ask students to define what stress means to them. Elicit examples from the class and chart on the whiteboard or computer.
IV. In pairs or small groups, have students group the stressors into categories. On a T chart, have students list healthy and unhealthy ways of reacting to stress.

V. Display the Cognitive Behavioral Model chart and walk students through an example (e.g., Situation: You stayed up late to study hard for a test and you received a failing grade. Thoughts: "I'm not smart. I'll never be able to learn this stuff!" Emotions: Sadness, depression, anxiety. Behavior: Asking a counselor if you can drop the class).

VI. Think and Write: Have students reflect on an experience they wish they had handled differently. Students chart the situation, their thoughts, emotions, and behaviors.

VII. Supportive Friends Protocol (adapted from Critical Friends Protocol):
  (A) In small groups of four or five, one volunteer shares their dilemma (e.g., a situation that brought about negative thoughts, emotions, and resulted in negative behaviors).
  (B) The other members of the group ask clarifying questions that can be answered with yes, no, or a simple explanation.
  (C) Each member of the group writes a deeper, probing question on a Post-it. The probing question should not give advice, suggestions, or be judgmental. For example, a good probing question would be: "I wonder how you would feel if someone you respect told you that you're good at ____?" We want to avoid probing questions like, "Why don't you change the way you think and stop being negative?" Aim for supportive questions.
  (D) The students hand over the sticky notes. The volunteer reads each one silently then chooses the one or two that *speak to them* most strongly. Read the questions selected. The student does not need to answer the questions; they simply need to reflect and share their thoughts about the question(s).
  (E) The volunteer listens silently while the other students in the group discuss the situation (i.e., sharing their thoughts and ideas for how the volunteer could handle the situation in alternative ways). Group should talk to each other and not direct their comments or discussion to the volunteer.
  (F) Finally, the volunteer shares what they heard and felt from the conversation including, but not limited to, ideas that might help them in the future.

VIII. Close the circle—Students return to the circle. Students share what they might do to calm down from an upsetting situation.

Assessment—Students write a short journal entry about a time when they have been able to react positively in an upsetting situation.

Lesson 5: Empathy and Compassion

Topic: Students will understand what another person is feeling and understand the other person's perspective as well as gain a more compassionate way to understand their own feelings (adding mindfulness and self-compassion to empathy and compassion).

Lesson Learning Outcomes
Students will
- be able to label emotions and feelings in themselves and in others.
- engage in active listening without expressing judgment or trying to solve or fix another person's problems.
- show self-empathy by using gentle curiosity to examine their own feelings.

(Continued)

Materials: Student journals; index cards.

Class Setup/Preparation: Move tables and chairs to make space for tablecloth in center of the circle, set up center of circle, write agenda on board, and display community agreements.

Activities:

I. Ring a bell; students meditate for twelve minutes. Ring a bell; students rest with eyes closed for three minutes.

II. Open the community circle. Check in with talking piece.

III. Play video clip "Please Hear What I'm Not Saying" by Charles Finn. Discuss with students how we don't always show how we are feeling and we sometimes wear masks.

IV. Empathy is the ability to understand another person's perspective and what another person might be feeling based on their lived experience. Some use the expression *to put oneself in another person's shoes* to describe empathy.

V. On an index card, students describe a problem or dilemma they are facing that they feel comfortable sharing in class.

VI. In small groups of four or five, students place their cards in the center of the circle. Each person selects a card that is not their own and presents the dilemma to the group as if it were their own issue. The group then discusses possible ways to handle the situation. Students should not reveal which card is theirs. In this way, students are able to learn empathy by experiencing what this problem might feel like to another person.

VII. Bring the whole class back together and debrief. What did it feel like to think about someone else's problem as your own?

VIII. Next, students return to their groups. Have two or three students volunteer to explain a situation for which they would like empathy (e.g., this could be a happy, sad, scary, or upsetting event). Once the student describes the situation, the other members of the group respond by asking "Are you feeling _____?" Then the volunteers share how they feel and reflect on how it felt to be listened to and to have others express in a caring way how they might be feeling.

IX. Close the circle—Students return to the circle. Students share what their emotion is in this moment.

Assessment—Over the next week, students will write in their journals a sentence or two each day about the emotions they experienced that day and how that impacted their mood and their interactions with family, friends, and peers.

Have students select an object (e.g., book, song, food, or clothing) that represents their culture. They should bring the object or a picture of it to school for the next lesson.

Lesson 6: Respect and Restorative Justice

Topic: Students will understand the importance of giving and receiving respect and how that builds trust in relationships. Students will demonstrate an awareness of their own cultural backgrounds and others' cultural backgrounds.

Lesson Learning Outcomes
Students will

- understand ways to show respect.
- understand what Restorative Justice is and be able to participate effectively in the process.
- be able to articulate their cultural practices and show appreciation for other cultures.

Materials: Student journals; students' cultural objects; cards for writing appreciation notes.

Class Setup/Preparation: Move tables and chairs to make space for tablecloth in center of the circle, set up center of circle, write agenda on board, and display community agreements.

Activities:

I. Ring a bell; students meditate for twelve minutes. Ring a bell; students rest with eyes closed for three minutes.

II. Open the community circle. Check in with talking piece.

III. Show Restorative Justice at Oakland's Fremont High. Ask students to describe how their experiences in community circles thus far have been and whether they are similar or different to those of the students in the video clip.

IV. Have students brainstorm respectful versus non-respectful actions in different settings (e.g., at home, in class, in the cafeteria, playing sports, in a club, at a cafe, or on the bus). Have a few volunteers act out a role-play of a respectful interaction and then the opposite. Discuss how the person who is disrespected might feel and how the observers might feel.

V. Use Restorative Justice questions and hold a circle to repair harm from the disrespectful interaction. For the person who acted disrespectfully: "What happened? What were you thinking about at the time? What have you been thinking about after the incident? Whom do you think might have been affected? What do you think you could do to make things right?" For the others: "What were you thinking when this happened? What effect has this incident had on you or others? What has been the hardest thing? What do you think needs to happen to make things right?"

VI. Ask students to think about how one person's definition of respect and disrespect could be different from another person's definition? Could this be tied to cultural differences? If so, how? How might your culture impact the ways in which you view the interaction in the previous activity.

VII. Now ask students to think about the objects they brought in that reflect their culture. Have students write about their cultural object answering the following questions: What is it? When is it used? What does it mean to them personally? Students share their objects and the personal significance with the class.

VIII. Close the circle—Students return to the circle. Students say one phrase about how they felt sharing taking part in the Restorative Justice circle.

Assessment—Each student writes *cards of appreciation* for three to five students in the class explaining what they learned and why it is important to them. The cards can be a way of saying thank-you for what they have learned from their peers.

Lesson 7: Intercultural Communication Skills

Topic: Students will understand that communication involves verbal and nonverbal cues. Gestures, facial expression, tone of voice, and attentive listening, all have an impact on communication.

Lesson Learning Outcomes
Students will

- understand the difference between verbal and nonverbal communication.
- demonstrate gestures, facial expression, and tone of voice to communicate effectively.
- pay attention to patterns of participation and whose voice is being heard.

Materials: Student journals.

Class Setup/Preparation: Move tables and chairs to make space for tablecloth in center of the circle, set up center of circle, write agenda on board, and display community agreements.

Activities:

I. Ring a bell; students meditate for twelve minutes. Ring a bell; students rest with eyes closed for three minutes.

II. Open the community circle. Check in with talking piece.

III. Explain the telephone game to students. One person writes a sentence down, then whispers it to the person beside them. This continues until the end of the line. The last person says the sentence out loud. The class discusses how the message changed.

IV. Next, have the class play charades in groups of four or five students. Debrief by asking if the message was conveyed and how it was transmitted. Was the message delivered effectively?

V. Who's talking? Before the next set of activities involving class discussion, quietly ask two students of different race and gender to observe and keep track of who is speaking and how often. Instruct them to have at least four categories: person of color/female; person of color/male; white female; and white male. They may also want to take notes on communication styles (e.g., talking over another person, interrupting, not speaking, backing down, or arguing).

VI. Ask several students to volunteer to show a scene from a favorite show in which two people are in conversation. Ask them to find examples of clear and effective communication and have at least one student find a scene where communication breaks down.

VII. Show the video clips and have a class discussion about what the *effective communicators* did well and what led to the miscommunication in the other scene. Elicit observations about facial expressions, tone of voice, and gestures.

VIII. Provide examples from the two activities (telephone and charades) to show that what you want to communicate is not always what others understand. Ask students how this may result in rumors and gossip (e.g., someone tells someone a secret and it gets passed on and it gets changed and distorted).

IX. Introduce the concept of paying attention to patterns of participation to the whole class. Without judgment, elicit discussion based on questions such as the following: Who do you think talks the most? Who is quiet? What might it feel like to have your voice heard, respected, affirmed? What might it feel like to not have a voice? Debrief *Who's talking* by informing the class that we had a couple intelligence agents in class watching our patterns of participation. Ask the two students to report their observations. What was surprising? What was expected? What are ways we can interrupt typical patterns and how would that affect the atmosphere in the class?

X. Close the Circle—Students return to the circle. Students say what they learned about communication and how participation can come in many forms—for example, a quieter student may be saying a lot by being attentive and nodding when you talk.

Assessment—Students reflect on what surprised them from the lesson in their journals (e.g., patterns of participation and how communication breakdowns occur). Students write in their journals possible strategies for how to repair a communication breakdown they have recently experienced with a family member, friend, classmate, or teacher.

Lesson 8: Conflict Resolution

Topic: Students will understand the importance of being a part of the solution to the conflict or misunderstanding. Learn how to reframe or de-escalate arguments and have productive difficult conversations.

Lesson Learning Outcomes
Students will

- be able to use I-statements, speak from one's own perspective, and be aware of one's own and the other person's feelings and emotions when each is triggered.
- be able to use "soft starts and ends" to have difficult conversations.
- understand and be able to use gentle curiosity to reflect on another's perspective that is different than one's own.

Materials: Student journals

Class Setup/Preparation: Move tables and chairs to make space for tablecloth in center of the circle, set up center of circle, write agenda on board, and display community agreements.

Activities:

I. Ring a bell; students meditate for twelve minutes. Ring a bell; students rest with eyes closed for three minutes.

II. Open the community circle. Check in with talking piece.

(Continued)

III. Frame the Purpose of the Class

Conflict resolution means working out a problem or disagreement without fighting, running away or going against your feelings. Knowing how to handle conflicts in a positive way can help people stay safe from violence, feel good about themselves, and learn to respect others. Physical violence, name-calling, threats, bullying, teasing, and other forms of negative communication often escalate conflicts and lead to serious consequences, including physical injury, lowered self-esteem, and punishment. Good communication involves being a good listener, considering and respecting the other person's point of view, working together to think of solutions, and learning to relax the body and calm the mind during high tension situations. Practicing these positive communication skills can help people make responsible choices during high-tension situations and avoid violence and further problems. (San Diego County District Attorney, Project Roots)

IV. IN-TWO-OUT activity

(A) IN: Have students write a couple of sentences about a time they were in an argument or disagreed with someone close to them describing only the facts, leaving out emotionally charged words. Next, from the *other person's perspective*, have the students in pairs share their answers to the following questions: What caused the issue? What are you (from the other's perspective) feeling? What needs to happen to resolve the conflict (again thinking from the other person's perspective)?

(B) Teach techniques to handle conflicts and stay connected. First, take a deep breath exhaling slowly. Ask yourself, what is my goal? What is in the best interest of this relationship? Is what I am about to say going to escalate or de-escalate the conflict? Then, consider how to present your concerns. In a gentle, calm manner, use a soft start, present the concern, and acknowledge the other person's feelings. Explain as directly as possible what you need to move forward. Use a "soft end" to say what you hope for in the relationship. For example, "I value our friendship. I feel hurt when you talk behind my back. I need you to consult me first before you talk about me with other people. I want us to continue being friends."

(C) TWO: In pairs, students practice *soft start* and *soft end* difficult conversations. Have students brainstorm times when they have felt hurt, triggered, overlooked, and the like. Write their ideas on the board. Then have students sign up in pairs to role-play one scenario each using the *soft start* and *soft end* method.

(D) OUT: Have several pairs volunteer to role-play in front of the class for feedback. As students listen and watch the role-play, ask them to look for *two glows and one grows* (i.e., two things they liked and one thing that could be improved).

V. Close the Circle—Students return to the circle. Students share what they might do differently when trying to have a difficult conversation with a friend or family member.

Assessment—Reflecting on all eight lessons, students should write in their journals about what actions they would like to put into practice. What skills have they learned that they would like to incorporate into their daily lives?

CONCLUSION

Each of these lessons reinforces a humanistic approach to SEL and is rooted in anti-racist pedagogy. Deficit thinking is one of the most dominant forms of racism in education. Educators should honor and validate the assets students bring with them to class each day. As described in Community Cultural Wealth theory, each student possesses their own unique cultural, linguistic, navigational, familial, aspirational, social, and resistant capital (Yosso, 2005).

These assets are at the forefront of the learning objectives in the lessons. As students move through the progression of the lesson sequence, they gain skills in self-awareness; learn how to understand and appropriately interpret their emotions; express empathy, compassion, and respect for their peers and themselves; and explore ways to communicate effectively and repair harm with people from diverse cultures and backgrounds.

REFERENCES

Camangian, Patrick. "Social and Emotional Learning is Colorblind Hegemony: Proposing a Pedagogy & Psychology of Humanization Instead." Presentation at the 2018–2019 Speaker Series on Race, Inequality and Language in Education, Stanford University, Graduate School of Education, February 20, 2019.

Ginwright, Shawn. *Hope and Healing in Urban Education: How Urban Activists and Teachers are Reclaiming Matters of the Heart*. New York: Routledge, 2016.

Goleman, Daniel. *Emotional Intelligence: Why It Can Matter More than IQ*. New York: Bantam Books, 2005.

Lipton, Bruce. *The Biology of Belief: Unleashing the Power of Consciousness, Matter and Miracles*. Santa Rosa, CA: Elite Books, 2005.

Nidich, Sanford, Rainforth, Maxwell, Haaga, David, Hagelin, John, Salerno, John, Travis, Fred, Tannerm Melissa, Gaylord-King, Carolyn, Grosswald, Sarina, and Schneider, Robert. "A Randomized Controlled Trial on Effects of the Transcendental Meditation Program on Blood Pressure, Psychological Distress, and Coping in Young Adults." *American Journal of Hypertension 22* (2009): 1326–1331.

Obama, Barack. *White House Report: The Continuing Need to Rethink Discipline*. Washington, D.C.: Executive Office of the President, 2016.

Orme-Johnson, David and Barnes, Vernon. "Effects of the Transcendental Meditation Technique on Trait Anxiety: A Meta-Analysis of Randomized Controlled Trials." *The Journal of Alternative and Complementary Medicine 20* (2014): 330–341.

Rodriguez, Victoria Christine, Hussain, Shadab Fatima, and Padilla, Amado. *Stress and Coping of English Learners in the 21st Century*. Charlotte, NC: Information Age Publishing, 2018.

Roeser, Robert and Peck, Stephen. "An Education in Awareness: Self, Motivation, and Self-Regulated Learning in Contemplative Perspective." *Educational Psychologist 44* (2009): 119–136.

Suárez-Orozco, Carola, Rhodes, Jean, and Milburn, Michael. "Unraveling the Immigrant Paradox: Academic Engagement and Disengagement among Recently Arrived Immigrant Youth." *Youth & Society 41* (2009): 151–185.

Tong, Virginia. "Understanding the Acculturation Experience of Chinese Adolescent Students: Sociocultural Adaptation Strategies and a Positive Bicultural and Bilingual Identity." *Bilingual Research Journal 37* (2014): 83–100.

Wendt, Staci, Hipps, Jerry, Abrams, Allan, Grant, Jamie, Valosek, Laurent, and Nidich, Sanford. "Practicing Transcendental Meditation in High Schools: Relationship to Well-being and Academic Achievement among Students." *Contemporary School Psychology 19* (2015): 312–319.

Yosso, Tara. "Whose Culture Has Capital? A Critical Race Theory Discussion of Community Cultural Wealth." *Race Ethnicity and Education 8* (2005): 69–91.

INTERLUDE BY JANE BLEASDALE

This chapter reflects the work of Margaret Peterson and the journey she is on. It was a pivotal moment in Margaret's professional development, her insights into a student's social emotional learning, that informed her understanding of humanism and the deep impact human bias and privilege can and does have on education. As educators read into humanistic social and emotional learning, they discover the internal world that frames the rising digital native generations. In Chapter 4, Nicole Cuadro highlights the essentials for understanding digital ethics and how to infuse them into every classroom.

NOTE

1. Professor Patrick Camangian challenges educators to examine the social emotional learning construct through a lens of humanization. Specifically, educators must address with intentionality the systemically imposed self-loathing, divide and conquer mentality, and sub-oppression by teaching students to gain knowledge of self, solidarity, and self-determination (Camangian, 2019).

Chapter 4

Teaching Digital Ethics

Nicole M. Cuadro

The awareness and importance of digital ethics is growing everyday as the use of technology grows throughout our world. If students do not become aware of the significance of digital ethics at the high school level, they may lack the professional and personal skills necessary to complete routine tasks within digital spaces. These lessons go far beyond behavioral issues, and they provide meaningful activities and reflections that supports professional and personal growth in the field of digital ethics.

The internet has evolved into a participatory space where students can connect, collaborate, and create content with a global audience. With the use of technology in the classroom becoming more prevalent, educators and students alike must work to promote a respectful and ethical use of technology. While many schools have adopted Acceptable Use Policies to ensure appropriate technology usage at school, the significance of digital ethics spans far beyond the classroom. In this *unit design*, teachers find digital learning exercises which support students practice of professional and ethical behavior.

Unit Learning Outcomes

Students will

- critically explore the importance of their individual digital identity, and how their identity may impact their future.
- become creative communicators, who create work ethically utilizing digital tools and platforms.
- recognize and cultivate their roles and responsibilities as digital citizens as they navigate through local and global digital societies.

Chapter 4

FOUNDATIONAL DIGITAL ETHICS

Lesson 1: Digital Identity
Lesson 2: Digital Footprint
Lesson 3: Ethical Online activity
Lesson 4: Digital Communication
Lesson 5: Intellectual Property
Lesson 6: Digital Privacy and Security
Lesson 7: Web Content Authenticity

Lesson 1: Digital Identity

Lesson Learning Outcomes
Students will

- become aware of digital identities that exist
- discuss why people may choose to identify as someone other than themselves in an online setting

Introduction
Digital identities vary greatly. Some individuals create online characters that closely resemble what they actually look like. Others create avatar identities that differ greatly from their actual identity.

Brainstorm
Students will begin the lesson by brainstorming (aloud, while teacher transcribes on the board) ways in which they identify themselves in digital spaces.

Central Activity. Your Digital Identity

1. *All Students View: NY Times Avatar Slideshow:* https://www.nytimes.com/slideshow/2007/06/15/magazine/20070617_AVATAR_SLIDESHOW_index/s/17avat.1.ready.html
2. THINK. PAIR. SHARE. (Partners)
    a. What are some identity differences you noticed throughout the slideshow? (Gender, superhero, barbarian)
    b. Why might someone decide to disguise themselves as a different gender/character/etc. in an online setting?
    c. What are some advantages/disadvantages of disguising yourself as someone other than yourself in an online setting?

Wrap-Up: Digital Identity Discussion: (whole class)

Discussion questions:

1. If you were to create an avatar for yourself, what would it look like?
2. What is your impression of the digital identities shown in the slideshow?
3. Should you trust individuals that are presenting themselves in the form of an avatar?

Lesson 2: Digital Footprint

Lesson Learning Outcomes
Students will
- analyze their online and offline identity/representation
- cultivate their online identity (digital footprint) in a safe, and ethical fashion

Introduction
Explain goals for the day and orient students to what they are learning.

Central Activity
Your Digital Footprint & Why it Matters!

Scenario
You are about to interview for the Summer internship of your dreams at a local technology start up. During an information session, the hiring manager for the company shares that they have a policy of completing a digital footprint audit/search as a part of their background check process. In order to prepare for this process, you will conduct a digital footprint self-evaluation to research whether you are making a *professional* digital impression.

Directions for Digital Footprint Self-Evaluation
1. Open your most commonly used web browser and make sure you are signed out of all of your social media accounts. Also, clear *all* browsing data for your browser.
2. Go to the sites listed and search your name (first and last)
   a. Google Search: https://www.google.com/advanced_search
   b. Facebook Search: https://www.facebook.com/search.advance/
   c. Twitter Search: https://twitter.com/search-advanced
   d. Instagram Search: https://help.instagram.com/1482378711987121
   e. LinkedIn Search: https://www.linkedin.com/help/linkedin/answer/302/searching-on-linkedin?lang=en
3. For each site, indicate (*Yes or No*) whether or not you were able to find yourself.
4. Look closely at the content you were able to locate for each site, make notes about your "professional" digital footprint impression. Pay close attention to the following:

   Achievements
   a. Hobbies listed
   b. Language usage (typos, slang, swear words, offensive language)
   c. Images
   d. Personal Information (address, phone number, email, location)
   e. Once you have completed your observations and notes taking, consider the following:
   Does my digital footprint portray who I really am in a professional way?
   Describe (taking your best guess) what your employer's impression might be based on what you were able to find.

(Continued)

Wrap-Up Activity. Digital Footprint Journal, Pair, Share
Students write a journal entry answering the questions below.

Discussion Questions

1. What was your impression of your digital footprint? (Were you surprised or caught off guard by anything you found?)
2. Does your digital footprint show positive, safe, ethical and legal behavior?
3. What type of information would you want an employer to see about you online?
4. What type of information would you NOT want an employer to see about you online?
5. How does your digital footprint which you share with your friends (on social media) differ from the person you want your future employers to see?
6. If you want to change your digital footprint, how would you go about doing that?

2- Students will work with a partner to discuss their findings.

3- Students will share as a whole group any interesting findings or commonalities.

Lesson 3: Ethical Online Activity

Lesson Learning Outcomes
Students will

- identify types of cyberbullying
- demonstrate safe, ethical, legal, and positive behavior in online settings.

Introduction Activity

1. Provide each student with 7–10 Sticky Notes
2. Direct students to write down what they think cyberbullying is. Each sticky note should only include 1 example. (Maybe they've seen it happen or they've heard about it happening).
3. Collect sticky notes
4. With the help/input from students, collate and gather sticky notes according to different types of cyberbullying on a board of blank wall in the classroom
5. Teacher/Moderator points out significant themes that arise.

Central Activity: Role Play Activity-

Three Students Bullying in the Real World
Student 1- The victim: Walking down the street
   accidentally bumps into Student 2
Student 2- The Bully: Walking the opposite direction up the street
   S2: "Hey little loser, you're such a moron, watch where you're walking!"
   S2: Shoves S1 onto the ground, kicks S1 a few times
Student 3- The Bystander: Is walking by when the interaction of S1 + S2 occurs.
   S3: Intervenes when S2 begins kicking S1.
   S3: "HEY! STOP right now!"

Student 2- Has no idea there was anyone watching him, gets spooked and runs away as fast as he can.
Student 3- Walks up to S1 to make sure they're alright
    S3: "Are you alright?"
Student 1- Looks up at S3 in complete embarrassment
    S1: "Yea, I'm alright. Thanks for stopping that bully."
Whole class Activity- Create Cyberbullying Interaction Scripts: Work in groups of 2–3 to create a script of what this would look like in an online cyberbullying interaction.

Requirements

- Must include at least one of each of the following characters (Victim, Cyberbully, Bystander)

Wrap-Up
Digital Cyber bullying Discussion: (whole class)

Discussion questions

1. What are some ways you, or someone you know has been a victim of cyberbullying?
2. What can you do (as a bystander) to stop cyberbullying when you see it happening?
3. Who are some of your most valuable resources when you or someone you know has been a victim of cyberbullying?
    - Online Cyberbullying Interaction must be realistic

Lesson 4: Digital Communication

Lesson Learning Outcomes
Students will

- write a concise and respectful email message
- evaluate email messages for proper grammar and spelling

Introduction Activity: 1-minute quick write

- Describe a time when you or a friend received a message online that was offensive or completely caught you off guard because of the tone.

Activity

1. Review **Netiquette:** The ethical and respectful way of communicating in a digital setting.

Tips for success: When you are communicating online, ask yourself the following questions:
Does it contain; a concise subject line, salutation, body of message, closure/signature?
Is the purpose of my email clearly stated?
Does my message have a respectful tone?
Are there any grammatical or spelling errors?

(Continued)

2. Give students the following scenario.

Email to the Superintendent.

Scenario: You are a member of the basketball team, which is currently in season. The Superintendent of your school district just sent out a memo to all members of the community stating that all basketball teams in the district will be cut from schools, effective immediately due to budget cuts. You have a lot on the line here, as you are expecting a visit from two college basketball recruiters.

3. Student task: Write a concise and respectful message to the Superintendent of Schools with clear arguments of why Basketball should not be cut. Your response include all necessary parts, and should be between 6–10 sentences.
4. Follow-up: Students swap email messages with one another and peer edit, for any grammar, spelling, or tone mistakes.

Wrap-Up: Whole Class discussion

1. Why should you always send concise and respectful messages?
2. What tools do you use to check your messages before they get sent?

Lesson 5: Rights and Obligations When Using and Sharing Intellectual Property

Lesson Learning Outcomes
Students will

- define Fair Use and Copyright policy
- demonstrate ethical debates regarding creative works

Introduction Activity

- Teacher read aloud to students: You have been assigned by your media teacher to create an original piece of music.
- 1 minute free write to answer the following question(s)
- Where and how will you gain inspiration for this project?

Activity

A. Review the following definitions with students

Copyright: Creative works by others are protected by copyright laws. In order to respect these laws legally and ethically, creators must follow these rules:

1. Figure out who owns the content
2. Gain permission to use the work
3. Purchase it
4. Provide credit to the original creator
5. Use the original creation responsibly

Fair Use: It may be legal (at times) to use creative works under the guidance of fair use. The following rules apply to Fair Use:

1. Only utilize a small amount of the original creation
2. Utilize creative material in a different way than originally intended
3. Never use someone else's creative works to make a profit

B. Musical Creativity Debate (2–3 large groups)
- There's a student in this class that believes remixing a song created by someone else is legal and ethical.
- Each group will craft an opening statement and main points for a debate on whether remixing music is legal and ethical.
- When groups are presenting, other students will take notes and be ready to argue with or agree with the statements being made.

Wrap-Up: Whole Class discussion

1. What can be said about the different perspectives on remixing someone else's work?
2. Why are ethical and legal rules put into place when it comes to creative work?
3. How might your decision to remix someone else's work (without permission) effect a musician?

Lesson 6: Digital Privacy and Security

Lesson Learning Outcomes
Students will

- evaluate privacy and security for both real-world and online settings
- determine the consequences of a breach in digital privacy.

Introduction Activity

- Discuss with a partner should employers be able to review your online activity during school/work hours?

Central Activity

1. Review the following definitions

    - Privacy options: a website may provide an option regarding what it does with your information
    - Third party: A company or person that is not you or the original owner of a website
    - Cookies: small text files on your computer placed by websites to collect information about your system and browsing history.

2. Share the following story: You have just started a new internship at a local startup. You receive a notification that the company has hired a third-party consultant to observe the daily experience that happens at your office for one week. They will track seat time, the amount of times you leave your seat, where you go when you leave your seat, as well as all the websites you visit throughout your day. At the end of that week, the third-party consultant will provide a report with data on daily life at your company to the CEO of the company.

3. Think/Pair/Share: Jot down a few initial ideas you have about this data collection. What questions or concerns do you have? Pair up with a partner and role play the conversation. One of you plays the role of the employer who is pro data collection—the other is the employee who sees this as an invasion of privacy.

(Continued)

Wrap-Up

Whole class discussion:

- Who else (besides the CEO) might gain access to this data?
- Should this data be completely private? How can you be 100% sure it's private?
- Should employees be able to review the data about themselves?

Lesson 7: Web Content Authenticity

Lesson Learning Outcomes
Students will

- evaluate websites for content authenticity
- analyze problems and consequences associated with fake news

Context

As this is also perceived as 'political issue' teachers are encouraged to review the context before jumping into the first activity.

As educators, we need to be keenly aware that not all content on the internet is true. Whether students are asked to conduct a simple search or an expansive research report, it is extremely crucial that they learn ways to tell if web content is written factually, accurately and is free of bias. This activity will ask students to evaluate several websites which are masked as real, but are actually filled with misinformation. These fictional websites will provide students with an understanding that not everything you read online is authentic.

Introduction Activity

Quick write: Where do you go to find information for projects? How long does it take to find the information you are looking for?

Central Activity: Website Evaluation Activity

1. Analysis Inquiry Description:

For each website visited, the students will complete a three-part analysis inquiry (see below). The following questions should be asked before starting the evaluation activity:

Who is the author of this content?

What are 2–3 interesting facts you learned from this website?

Is this website credible and without bias?

2. (Individually or in pairs) Students will visit the following websites and fill out the corresponding Analysis Inquiry:

Pacific Northwest Tree Octopus: http://zapatopi.net/treeoctopus

All About Explorers: http://allaboutexplorers.com

Dog Island: http://www.thedogisland.com

Wrap-Up
Many of the students will begin to realize that this content is not factual pretty quickly. Other students may not fully grasp it right away. After everyone has *completed* their *analysis inquiry, have them turn in their work. Once all work has been collected, state to the class that each one of those websites was fake and that none of the content in those pages can be deemed credible. Follow up with a discussion about fake news.

Consider the following questions:
- Why is content credibility important?
- What are some consequences of fake news or biased content?

CONCLUSION

Learning digital ethics, being self and socially aware in the digital landscape, includes a great deal of personal and communal reflection and content analysis. By reflecting on one's personal ethical use of digital spaces, the student becomes deeply aware of the significance and potential implications involved in ethical/unethical practices in digital spaces. Content analysis gives personal and group reflection an informed and critical edge. Large and small group discussions open spaces that expand the parameters of reflections—students discover digital social agency and responsibility.

As educators, there is great significance in teaching digital ethics to your students, regardless of your field of study. The instructional praxis in this chapter can be adapted to and shared within any subject matter. The practice of digital ethics is invaluable for students as they enter their adult lives in a highly digital world. The digital world is a vast and sometimes daunting space, by providing students with the opportunity to develop personal and professional digital ethical skills teachers are setting them up for success in these spaces.

REFERENCES

"Double Agents" slideshow in *The New York Times Magazine*. June 15, 2007. https://www.nytimes.com/slideshow/2007/06/15/magazine/20070617_AVATAR_SLIDESHOW_index/s/17avat.1.ready.html accessed 2019.

INTERLUDE BY JANE BLEASDALE

Call this generation—*digital natives, cradle techies*: they have far more digital opportunities and skills than we imagined even a decade ago. Few of us have truly understood and embraced the opportunities of digital learning—but Nicole Cuadro is one of the few. From 5th grade classrooms to higher education instruction, Nicole exemplifies best practices in the area of digital learning. Her experience is steeped in an ethical embrace of all that is good in the digital world with a healthy awareness of the challenges. The instructional intention is for all learners to embrace digital learning as an opportunity to promote the common good.

Austin Pidgeon bridges ever-growing moral divides between paper and digital texts in a traditional English Literature classroom setting. He sets directions that bridge the ever-growing divide.

Chapter 5

Espousing Equity and Inclusion in an English Class: A Unit Plan for a Literature Class in Secondary Education

Austin Pidgeon

This unit suggests strategies for literature teachers to create an equitable and inclusive curriculum that affords students the opportunity to consider their individual and collective identities, focusing primarily on the role that race/ethnicity plays in identity development. Exploring a variety of literary texts from diverse mediums, students focus on multiple perspectives of various topics that center the voices of those most often underrepresented in mainstream society. They will work together toward a greater understanding of the lived experiences of the characters they encounter and the classmates they encounter them with.

Unit Title: Espousing Equity and Inclusion in an English Class: Exploring Literature through the Lenses of Immigration, Stereotyping, and Identity Development

INTRODUCTION AND RATIONALE

It is evident that mere academic pursuit is not sufficient in leveling what is still a tragically lopsided playing field in American society. Rather, education needs to operate in both an intellectual and a moral framework. In order to be considered true practitioners of ethical pedagogy, educators should work to build an inclusive culture in their classrooms that centers the voices of students on the margins, that demands equal opportunity for student voice and success, and that affirms the various lived experiences of what is an increasingly diverse student population in schools today.

Teachers should challenge students to consider their relative privilege in school settings (as well as outside of them), to build authentic community with their peers by engaging them as individual persons with dignity, to allow for tension in disagreement as conducive to personal and collective growth, and to move beyond tolerance and toward inclusivity or belonging. This can be accomplished in both instruction and curriculum. Literature classes, in particular, offer unique and fruitful settings for conducting this work.

Reading lists should be culturally relevant to your students and be reflective of your specific school context but should also show a preference for narratives by and about people traditionally understood to be on the margins of society. Such preferential option in curriculum is precisely the moral framework required in our ethical pursuit toward this much needed positive change in society.

UNIT LEARNING OUTCOMES

At the end of this unit, students will be able to

- identify the main subject of a text.
- identify the central conflict of a text.
- illustrate basic understanding of the concept of examining texts through *lenses*.
- harness textual evidence to support an original argument.
- examine literary texts through the specific *lenses* of immigration, stereotypes, and identity development (social awareness).
- examine their own identity development through the *lense*s of immigration and stereotypes (self-awareness).
- connect personal experience to the experience(s) of a character in a text.
- analyze the impact of race/ethnicity on identity development.
- identify similarities in the experiences of various authors, characters, and classmates (social awareness).
- express similarities in the experiences of various authors, characters, and classmates.
- examine literary themes in different texts (e.g., songs, poems, and articles).
- illustrate understanding of the concept of *allusion* in literature.
- compose an original argument of literary analysis.
- peer revise an original argument of literary analysis.
- make edits to a writing sample based on peer feedback.

Lesson 1: How Do We Read? Examining Texts through Literary Lenses

Topic:

This first lesson offers students an introduction to the core concepts at play in this unit and allows space for some initial reflection on students' identities in the context of race/ethnicity. The unit utilizes *an anchor text*—here, the graphic novel *American Born Chinese* by Gene Luen Yang—to set the context of identity exploration and then supplements discussion with smaller texts of various mediums to add breadth and depth to the discourse. Ask students to read the anchor text prior to the first day of the unit (it's short!).

They will read the supplemental texts along the way. Again, choose texts that are culturally relevant to your students and appropriate for your specific school context (e.g., region, grade level, greater school community, etc.). This unit offers a list of supplemental texts of various mediums, though, just as with the anchor text, the instructor should feel free to swap out texts as they see fit.

Lesson Learning Outcomes
Students will

- identify the main subject of a text.
- identify the central conflict of a text.
- illustrate basic understanding of the concept of examining texts through *lenses*.
- harness textual evidence to support an original argument.

Activities:

- Students will begin class with a small group discussion. To facilitate making space for all students to participate in this discussion, regardless of their willingness to share out loud in the large group setting, arrange students in groups of three and ask the following, one question at a time:

  (1) What are your *initial reactions* to the story? Here, anything goes. Students may discuss the plot, themes, the writing style, specific characters, or something else. Allow free range of thought and make sure all students are contributing. To facilitate this, consider offering sixty-second blocks of time for each student to serve as the sole speaker. Encourage the speaker to share freely and not worry about where their thoughts may lead them.

  At the end of each block, the speakers' groupmates can spend a few moments reacting to the speaker's comments before the teacher starts the next sixty-second block of time and asks a different student to serve as the speaker. Ensure all students have equal airtime in these discussions and that no one student is dominating conversation by actively walking around from group to group, listening (and potentially redirecting) but not interrupting the students' discourse. Here, student participation means both talking when it is their turn as speaker and intentionally listening when it is not.

  Allow three to four minutes for students to share and respond to these initial reactions.

  (2) What would you suggest is the *main subject* of the story? Students might ask what is meant by subject. Let them figure this out on their own. But again, make sure all students are contributing by using the same sixty seconds speaker method. Roam from group to group, listen in to students' answers, and, when appropriate, ask them to identify evidence from the text that supports their ideas. Allow three to four minutes for students to speak and react.

(Continued)

(3) What would you say is the *central conflict* of the story? Students may again ask what is meant by *central conflict*. Allow them to work this out together. Float from table to table, and ensure students are utilizing textual evidence to support their thoughts. Utilize the same sixty seconds speaker method again, or if you feel students are generating thoughtful conversation and appropriately sharing the mantle, ask them to simply dialogue together without restraint. In this case, intentional listening would be an appropriate form of participating throughout the discussion time. Allow three to four minutes for students to dialogue.

- Teachers should return the class to a large-group discussion and ask students to share some of their answers. Allow the conversation to wander where it may but make sure to dig into the text as students offer textual evidence in support of their comments. The focus should be on gathering insight into student understanding of the text thus far and discovering what details from the text they latch onto.
- Teachers can leverage this student knowledge later on in the unit. You may also want to ensure students' understanding of the subject and central conflict and consider offering some recourse depending on what students offer.
- Transition to some notetaking where students can explore some of the core concepts of the unit. (Depending on your school context, culture, and available resources, this can take multiple forms: handwritten notes in a three-ring binder, notes in a running Google Doc on a personal computer, or whatever else may work best for you. The unit does ask that students work consistently each day in the same notebook.)
- In particular, discuss the idea of reading texts through *lenses*. A *lens* in this context is simply a specific framework of thinking—maybe a theme, maybe an idea connected to the charism or guiding philosophy of your school, or maybe something else—through which the class will read, understand, and write about the text. When examining a text through specific lenses, students should seek out passages and ideas from the text that speak to each lens and teachers should navigate conversation toward these as well. It is useful to offer three lenses, in precise order, each with its own intention. Ask students to write these down in their notebooks below the entries from the previous discussion:

(1) The *primary lens* should be that which is most specific to the text at hand and applies to some people. The purpose here is to center the unique experience of the characters in the text. For example, in the case of *American Born Chinese*, offer the primary lens of *immigration* or, more precisely in this case, *the first-generation American experience*. This centers the first-generation experience, allowing those in the class who identify with this experience to speak confidently and with firsthand knowledge about this lens.

Make sure not to isolate any one or two students as ambassadors of this experience charged with speaking on behalf of their community but do try to affirm their experience and invite those students to serve as experts in the field, leading their peers in understanding of what it is like to, say, in this case, grow up as a first-generation American. If no students do or choose to identify with this experience, the class can still take some time unpacking what they know about this experience.

The idea is to center, to affirm, and to normalize an experience that many might consider a marginal one. Allow time for quick small-group discussion to unpack this lens.

(2) The *secondary lens* is one that can be applied more broadly. While not everyone can identify as a first-generation American, *most* people can understand the concept of combating stereotypes about themselves or their communities. Offer the secondary lens of *challenging stereotypes*. Allow students time to consider what stereotypes they are labeled with.

Is their student body stereotyped? Is their gender, sexual orientation, or race/ethnicity stereotyped? Is there a stereotype associated with their religious preference or their age? Allow time for quick small-group discussion to unpack these.

(3) The *tertiary lens* should be one that applies to *all* people. While only *some* people may claim to be first-generation Americans and only *most* people exert effort battling stereotypes, *all* people experience the desire to know who they are. Offer the tertiary lens of *identity development*. Ask students to consider what makes them who they are, and what events, ideas, hobbies, qualifiers, and other attributes or ideas go into their understanding of their own identities. Allow time for quick small-group discussion to unpack these.

- Remind students that their understanding of these concepts may be limited right now but that it's only day one and they will have plenty of time to continue to explore and unpack these concepts.
- Also note that the ethical dimension of these *lenses* is twofold: first, working with *lenses* allows students personal freedom of interpretation when examining literary texts while maintaining a group task of working together to investigate a few overarching ideas throughout a single text. This empowers each student to find unique meaning in the stories they encounter and helps to improve their reading comprehension and critical thinking skills while maintaining a group task that encourages students to work collaboratively toward a common goal.
- Second, as related to the notion of *inclusive human flourishing*, the choice of the specific *lenses* offered here aids in this work by encouraging students to examine who they are, how they relate to each other, and how they may limit their understanding and appreciation of others through stereotyping. In doing so, perceived and real interpersonal differences, which often act as barriers to connection for young people, are demystified for students as they gain confidence in understanding of who they are and who their peers are. This is precisely the intellectual and moral framework suggested in this chapter's introduction.
- In closing, transition students to their homework assignment, listed in the following section.

Assessment:

- Students should open their notebooks used during class, review the notes they took, and then respond to the following prompt:
  o Review, in particular, the three lenses from discussion today: *first-generation immigrant experience*, *challenging stereotypes*, and *identity development*. Explore your own identity through these lenses. Offer one brief, informal paragraph (six to ten sentences) of writing per lens:
    (1) In your first paragraph, explore your life through the concept of *immigration* or, if it applies to you, *the first-generation American experience*. Here are some questions to consider (you may answer some, or explore beyond these, but do not need to answer all): Are you a first-generation American immigrant? Where from? Where do you consider your *home*? Are you not a first-generation American? What generation, then? And where are your ancestors originally from? Or are you an indigenous member of our community? How does this affect your understanding of your own identity? How important is your ethnic heritage to you?

(Continued)

(2) In your second paragraph, explore the notion of *stereotypes* in your life. Here are some questions to consider: In what ways are you stereotyped? Why? How do you feel about these stereotypes? What do you do to challenge these stereotypes, if at all? Why? In what ways do you stereotype others?
(3) In your third paragraph, explore the idea of *identity development*. Here are some questions to consider: Especially in context of your previous answers, how do you define yourself? Why do you highlight these aspects of yourself? What experiences led to your understanding of your identity in this way? Explain in detail.

Lesson 2: How Do We Understand What We Read? Reinforcing Lenses and Close Reading

Topic:
This second lesson will ask students to build on their understanding of the three lenses offered in the first lesson, examining the anchor texts via those lenses in class and then applying that framework to a new supplemental text in their homework. Students will also continue their own self-examination in the process.

Lesson Learning Outcomes
Students will

- examine literary texts through the lenses of immigration, stereotypes, and identity development.
- examine their own identity through the lenses of immigration and stereotypes.
- analyze the impact of race/ethnicity on identity development.
- harness textual evidence to support an original argument (reinforced from previous lessons).

Activities:

- Students will begin class arranged in the same small groups as before. (These should remain consistent throughout this unit so that students can grow in their relationship with one another but should be changed for subsequent units so that each student has a chance to directly interact with each of their classmates at least a few times throughout a course.)
- This will go a long way toward building authentic community in class. Each will earn the opportunity to both interact with and know each of their peers, and each student will also earn the opportunity to share of themselves with their classmates in more intimate, personal ways than is allowed in a large group setting. This helps all students work toward a common flourishing.
- Begin class by having students share their homework responses in their small groups. Again, encourage equal airtime. Let students know they should not feel forced to share any details they are not comfortable disclosing with classmates or teacher and float the room to ensure active participation by all students. Allow five or six minutes for discussion.
- Return students to the large group and ask for volunteers to share their responses. This is a great opportunity to affirm student experience and identity. It is an especially good opportunity to center the experiences of those who identify with the primary lens, *first-generation American experience*. If a student does share their identification with this lens, ask permission to probe. What's it like for them? When did they learn of this? How do they feel their classmates perceive them because of this element of their identity? How important is this fact to the student's understanding of who they are? Let the conversation go where it may but try to limit the conversation to roughly ten to fifteen minutes. And again, affirm and center these voices but do not isolate any one student as a representative voice of a larger group.

- Transition into a close reading of the anchor text, *American Born Chinese*. Spend about fifteen to twenty minutes reading specific passages from the first half of the text evocative of the major themes. Remind students to focus only on the three lenses:
  (1) Where does the reader gain insight into the protagonist's experience as a *first-generation American*? Read some of these passages together. How or what does the protagonist initially feel about this? Is he ashamed or proud of this? Does he choose to express this or hide this element of his identity? Why might he feel the way he does? How do other characters treat him in relation to his identity as a first-generation American?
  (2) Where do we see evidence of *stereotyping* at play in the text? Read some of these passages together. Which characters are stereotyped? For what reason? And what effect does this have on the characters?
  (3) Where do you see the characters exploring their *identities*? Read some of these passages together. What moments in the text aid in their identity development? Are these positive or negative experiences? Why?
- In closing, have students continue their reflection via writing in the same notebook they have been working with (you may note that the instructor is the only one who may review their writing or you may suggest that you do not plan to read this at all—that it is simply a vehicle for their personal reflection. Either way, students should feel encouraged to write openly without being concerned about their peers reading their work). Have them answer the following prompt below their last written entry:

  How included do you feel in your school community? Why? Offer specific examples to illustrate your ideas.

Assessment:
- Students should finish up the writing prompt they began in class.
- Students should also actively read the article "Growing Up First Generation American: The 'In-Between' Identity" by Leslie Shakira Garcia (*Odyssey*, 2016), consider the three lenses as they read, and be prepared to discuss the article and their thoughts about it at the beginning of the next class.

Lesson 3: Who Are We, Really? Connecting Characters with Lived Experience

Topic:
This lesson reinforces students' ability to apply the theoretical frameworks of the lenses to texts of different mediums—here, an article and a poem. Students will naturally draw connections between what they have read in the anchor text and what they are reading in the supplemental texts. The emphasis should be on these comparisons, rather than on any contrasts.

Lesson Learning Outcomes
Students will
- connect personal experience to the experience(s) of a character in a text.
- examine literary texts through the lenses of immigration, stereotypes, and identity development (reinforced from previous lesson).
- analyze the impact of race/ethnicity on identity development (reinforced from previous lesson).
- harness textual evidence to support an original argument (reinforced from previous lessons).

(Continued)

Activities:
- Students should begin class by reviewing, in their small groups, the article from their homework. Ask a series of questions, one at a time, giving roughly one to two minutes per question:
  (1) What were your initial reactions to the article?
  (2) Where did you connect to the article? That is, do you share any of the same experiences as those mentioned by its author?
  (3) Where did you not connect to the article? That is, how has your experience differed from the author's experience?
  (4) What connections can you draw between the article and the book *American Born Chinese*?
- Return students to the large group and ask them to share what came up in their small-group discussion, one question at a time. Gauge the energy in the room and navigate the conversation accordingly but try to allow for around ten minutes for this discussion.
- Transition to have students actively read "Theme for English B" by Langston Hughes (*Poetry Foundation*). The poem explores, among other ideas, the concepts of *dual identity and code switching*, two ideas that are also present in *American Born Chinese*. Remind students to read the poem through the three lenses from yesterday: Where do they see the immigrant experience, or some version of it, at play (or not) in the poem? Where do they understand the concept of challenging stereotypes at play in this poem? And where do they see the speaker of the poem exploring their identity?
- Allow roughly five to eight minutes for students to actively read the poem. After this time, direct them to share their thoughts in small groups.
- Transition the class back to the large-group discussion. Have a couple of students take turns reading the poem aloud. Ask students if they'd like to share what they wrote in their annotations and make sure to give equal airtime to all students in class. If possible, project a copy of the poem and, as students offer comments and questions of analysis, write these down on the projected text. Students will feel empowered when they realize they have authority in interpreting these texts.
- Refrain from centering *a correct or best* reading of the piece (though you may want to highlight comments and questions that refer specifically to the given lenses); allow students to dictate the class's understanding of the text. Depending on the flow of conversation, consider exploring the following questions:
  (1) What is the subject of the poem?
  (2) What's the central conflict the speaker of the poem is experiencing? What evidence can you offer to support your answer?
  (3) How does the speaker understand their identity? What does the speaker *center*, or preference, by listing first? Why these attributes?
  (4) What part does race play in the speaker's musings?
  (5) How is the speaker's experience at their school similar to your experience at this school? How is it different?
- In closing, transition students into their homework assignment, listed in the following section.

Assessment:
- Students should continue their self-reflection process via a creative writing assignment. Drawing from class discussion about the poem, have students write their own version of the poem, highlighting similar themes and making sure to access the three lenses: the first-generation immigrant experience, the concept of challenging stereotypes, and the notion of identity development. Students should *mirror write* the piece—that is, they should utilize the same opening prompt from the poem (displayed in the following section), follow the same format and organizational structure, and explore similar topics.
- But, while the prompt, organization, and topics should be similar to the Hughes poem, the content of their *mirror writes* should be entirely unique to each student's lived experience; they should not fabricate. This is an opportunity for students to recall and reflect on their own experience and not to write imaginatively about someone else's, real or fictional. Students should begin their poem with the following prompt:

> "The teacher [or, insert your name!] said,
> *Go home and write*
> *a page tonight.*
> *And let that page come out of you—*
> *Then, it will be true.*
> I wonder if. . . ."

Lesson 4: What Connects Us? Comparative Studies in Literature

Topic:
Students will continue to unpack the lenses, today focusing primarily on the concept of stereotypes. While stereotypes tend to highlight that which differentiates us from one another based on certain identifiers, teachers should emphasize instead that which connects us.

Lesson Learning Outcomes
Students will

- identify similarities in the experiences of various authors, characters, and classmates.
- express similarities in the experiences of various authors, characters, and classmates.
- examine literary texts through the lenses of immigration, stereotypes, and identity development (reinforced from previous lessons).

Activities:

- Begin class by opening up space for students to share their creative *mirror writes* from the previous night. This should be a low pressure, positive environment for students to open up and share with and for their peers. Remind students that they will not be assessed on their pieces while sharing, that they do not need to have them memorized, and that they do not have to share if they do not want. But allow for some time for students to consider sharing.
- Once one student goes, many will likely follow. Take as long as you need to work through these. This can be as rich a learning moment as you allow it to be, and it can also go a long way toward building authentic community in class.

(Continued)

- Once everyone who would like to share has had the opportunity to do so, transition students to the poem "Human Family" by Maya Angelou (*All Poetry*). Instead of tasking students with actively reading this on their own, present it to the class and ask students to read in this way:

    Have one student read the first stanza, then have another student chime in (without having to raise their hand and be called on) to read the second stanza, and so on and so forth.

    When the class arrives at the last three stanzas, have all students in the class read together the phrase *we are more alike, my friends,/than we are unalike*.

- Enter into discussion with students about the content of the poem. Again, work through a series of questions. This time, though, simply ask the large group, one question at a time, and encourage equal airtime from all students in answering. Resist the urge to respond to each student or to provide your own interpretation of the poem. Center your students' voices. Consider asking (or, alternatively, you may have students quietly write out answers to some or all of these questions if you prefer):
    (1) What do you first or most notice about the poem?
    (2) What do you like about the poem?
    (3) What challenged you while reading the poem?
    (4) In what ways do we often "note the obvious differences" among people—maybe in the world at large, in our families, in our school community, or elsewhere? Be specific.
    (5) In what ways are *we more alike . . . than we are unalike*? Again, be specific.
    (6) Last, how does this poem relate back to other texts we have examined in this unit—*American Born Chinese*, "Growing Up First Generation American," "Theme for English B," your *mirror writes* of the same poem?
- Transition back to close reading of the anchor text, *American Born Chinese*. Focus primarily on the second lens of *stereotypes*. Select passages in which the protagonist and other characters from the text experience stereotyping. Unpack these scenes with your students, asking first for comprehension of the scenes and second about their critical response to them. And, as much as possible, relate the discussion back to the other texts offered throughout the unit.
- Introduce students to their homework assignment, listed in the following section.

Assessment:
- In your notebook answer the following prompt:
    o Look back to your *mirror write* poem. What types of personal identifiers did you offer in this piece? Did you mention your race, or age, or gender, or sexual orientation, or where you live, or something else? Reconsider each of those identifiers and informally answer: In what ways are you stereotyped based on these identifiers? In what ways do you stereotype others based on similar identifiers? Be honest and offer one paragraph per question.

Lesson 5: What Makes Us Who We Are? Considering the Third Lens of Identity Development

Topic:
Students will continue to unpack the lenses, focusing today primarily on the tertiary lens of identity development. Students will have gone through much analysis and reflection up to this point on the experiences and identities of both characters from literary texts and themselves. This lesson offers them the opportunity to formalize some of that discernment in consideration of a formal writing assignment to come.

Lesson Learning Outcomes
Students will

- examine literary themes in song.
- illustrate understanding of the concept of *allusion* in literature.

Activities:

- Begin class by allowing students to share in small groups what they wrote for homework the previous night. Ensure each student is speaking with equal airtime and float the room to engage students in what they've written. Allow about four to six minutes for this small-group discussion.
- Return students to the large group and ask them to share some of what was discussed in the small group. If they are comfortable with it, ask students to not share their own writing but relate to the large group what one of their small group members offered. This might leave some students feeling vulnerable, but this is a healthy tension and should add to the value of the classroom experience for them. This should also help build trust, which will help in your pursuit of building authentic community in class.
- Transition to a final text analysis, this time the song "History" by Yasiin Bey ft. Talib Kweli (produced by J. Dilla). First, show the visuals to the song in class. Ask students to pay attention to the many allusions offered in the music video. (They may have trouble keeping up with them, but you can unpack these with them later.) Once done, disseminate the lyrics of the song and ask students to quietly and actively read through them, focusing again on the three lenses. You can play the song once more while they do a quick read.
- Ask students to note where they see references to any potential immigrant experience, to any stereotyping, and to any process of identity development. Ask them to also note anything else that catches their attention.
- After giving students a few minutes to annotate the lyrics, have students briefly share in small groups what they noted in the song. Compare and contrast annotations on the three lenses, and have each student share with their partners what else caught their attention. Allow three or four minutes for this brief check-in.
- Next, turn their attention to the crowdsourced annotations of the song available on *Genius*. This is an ideal opportunity to discuss the concept of literary *allusions*, as these abound in the song. If there is time, and if you're up for it, work through these allusions one by one with students.
    o For example, in Yasiin Bey's opening verse, he notes that *he was born in a season where the world was quiet and cold/celebrations were going on*. This seems a simple reference to being born in the winter time, and the note about celebrations going on seems to reference, at least in this American context, maybe a Thanksgiving, Hanukkah, Christmas, New Year's Eve celebration, or something else. Ask students: Did they pick up on this? If so, which celebration did they consider this a reference to?
    o This can serve as a useful opportunity to discuss how readers bring their own experiences and identity into literary interpretation. A Christian student may have associated winter celebrations with Christmas; a Jewish student may have associated winter celebrations with Hanukkah; an agnostic student may have associated winter celebrations with New Year's Eve; and all American students in the classroom may have associated winter celebrations with Thanksgiving. Rather than focus on any *correct or best answer*, allow students to interpret freely and affirm their own meaning making in this process.

(Continued)

- After working through some of the other allusions in the song, focus back on the lenses, specifically the lens of identity development. Ask students the following questions:
  (1) How do the writers understand their own identities in this piece?
  (2) What role does the writers' generation (or when they were born) play in their identity development?
  (3) What role does socioeconomic status play in the identity development of the writers?
  (4) What role does their birthplace play in their identity development?
  (5) What else do the writers focus on in exploring their identities in this piece?
  (6) Last, Bey suggests that every soul has a *history* and that, *without understanding*, one *cannot proceed/complete*. What does he mean by this? And do you agree with this argument?
- Transition students to their homework assignment, listed in the following section.

Assessment:

- Yasiin Bey suggests that everyone has a history and that we must understand our history in order to *proceed complete*. Explore the narrative of one major character from *American Born Chinese*. What is this character's history, how does this character understand it, and how does this understanding allow the character to *proceed complete*? Utilize textual evidence to support your arguments. Offer one or two paragraphs in response.

Lesson 6: What Now? Expressing Original Arguments in Writing

Topic:
Students will reflect on the discussion and discernment they have practiced throughout this unit as preparation for producing an original argument of literary analysis that connects one of the literary lenses to two texts explored in this unit.

Lesson Learning Outcomes
Students will

- compose an original argument of literary analysis.
- harness textual evidence to support an original argument (reinforced from previous lessons).

Activities:

- Orient students in new groups based on which text they chose to write about for their homework assignment—*American Born Chinese*, "Growing Up First Generation American," "Theme for English B," "Human Family," or "History." Allow students a couple of minutes to briefly check in, reintroduce themselves, and get settled. If groups are too big or too lopsided, divide students into small groups of around three within each text selection.
- Ask students to share their responses with each other, focusing on their textual evidence of support. Again, encourage equal airtime for student sharing, float the room to ensure this and engage students, and allow five to seven minutes for this conversation.

- Return students to the large group and ask for some responses. At this point, students should be able to respond directly to each other without having to funnel questions and answers through the teacher. Consider sitting at eye level with the students (rather than standing behind a podium or sitting on an elevated chair). Ask students not to raise hands and not to make eye contact with the teacher but to directly engage each other in free flowing conversation, just as they have done each day in small groups. Feel free to step in to ask clarifying or probing questions but try to sit back and let the students lead and facilitate their own discussion here.
- When you feel students have demonstrated adequate understanding of the major ideas permeating the unit texts and have found useful textual evidence to support their arguments, return to a final close reading of the anchor text, *American Born Chinese*, and focus on the ending of the story. Choose specific passages that address this notion of identity development and allow students to unpack the ways in which the protagonist and other main characters come to a (more) complete understanding of who they are.
- Center race/ethnicity in this process. Seek connections to the various other texts students have examined during this unit. And remind students that they will need to express these connections in writing at the end of the unit and so now is the time to practice in their spoken comments.
- Introduce students to their final assessment: a formal writing assessment that asks students to analyze one of the lenses at play in the anchor text, *American Born Chinese*, and one other unit text of their choice. Give them the following prompt:

    In a 600- to 900-word essay, analyze one of the three lenses—the first-generation immigrant experience, combating stereotypes, or identity development—in the narratives of two major characters examined throughout the unit. You must write about a major character from the anchor text, *American Born Chinese*, and must write about one additional character from any other text examined throughout the unit. You should not write about two characters from the same text.

    Though this is a formal literary analysis essay and not a first-person or narrative essay, students should still draw from their personal reflections on their own identities throughout the unit in analyzing the characters in these texts. Probe with similar questions, put yourself in the shoes of the characters, and think about how each of the characters in question lives out the immigrant experience, battles stereotypes, or undergoes a unique process of identity development. Complete a first draft of this assessment before tomorrow's class.

Assessment:
- Students are to complete a first draft of their written assessment. They should be prepared to swap drafts with a classmate at the beginning of next class. Ideally, this writing assessment will build on the previous night's homework so students will already have some drafting done.

Lesson 7: Peer Revision and Writing Conferencing

Topic:
Students will peer review essays and spend time conferencing with each other to offer feedback on their writing. Students can also use class time to conference one on one with the teacher about their writing. This class should take the form of a writing workshop, and the teacher should be available as the students' needs.

(Continued)

Lesson Learning Outcomes
Students will
- peer revise an original argument of literary analysis.
- make edits to a writing sample based on peer feedback.

Activities:
- Students should start in their original small groups. Have each student rotate their paper (either by exchanging e-mail messages or by swapping paper copies) clockwise to a classmate next to them. Students will go through two rounds of revision and can follow the same sequence for each round.
- Students should read their classmate's paper three times. The first time through, students should read start to finish without stopping to comment. This first time through, students should simply try to understand the main argument, to get a feel for the organization of the paper, and to take stock of the component parts (e.g., title, essay, and works cited page). Again, students do not need to mark anything in this initial read. Allow roughly six to eight minutes for this.
- The second time through, students should stop to comment on three major areas of essay writing: the main argument (Is it clear? sound? original? argumentative?), the use of textual evidence of support (Are the details introduced with context? effectively illustrative of the argument? properly formatted? properly cited?), and the organization of the essay (Does each paragraph have a clear topic sentence? a clear main point? a transitional statement at the end of each paragraph?). Students should actively comment on the essay, noting aspects of each of these areas that are both strong and in need of development. Allow roughly eight to twelve minutes for this.
- The third time through, students should focus on the surface-level writing: Is the essay free from grammatical errors? How is the word choice? Does the writing flow well? Are there any issues in formatting that should be addressed? Is there anything else you notice about the essay that should be complimented or could be improved upon. Allow roughly four or five minutes for this.
- After students have worked through their third reading, have students swap their essays clockwise once more, then repeat the same sequence. It is okay for students to see what their peers have offered by way of feedback.
- After each student has read and revised two essays, have students return all copies to their original authors. Have students spend a few minutes conferencing in small groups. Each group should focus on one student at a time. The author in focus can attentively listen while their two groupmates spend a couple of minutes explaining what the essay did well and where the essay could be improved upon. After their peers have discussed their essay and the feedback on it, and as time permits, the author may ask for the peers to elaborate, or clarify, or offer further feedback.
- Allow about three or four minutes for conferencing, then have the group switch to focus on another student-author. Repeat this sequence a third time so that each student has a chance to hear from their peers.
- Once all students have had a chance to conference with their small groups about their essay, return the students to the large group and answer any questions the class may have regarding the details of the assessment, any common errors that came up in the peer revision process, or anything else they might need help with. Depending

on how much time is left, direct them to quietly work on their essay revisions and use the remainder of class to make yourself available for one-on-one conferencing with any student who needs additional help.
- Remind students when their writing assessment is due.

Assessment:
- Complete the writing assessment by its due date (up to teacher discretion).

CONCLUSION

The close and careful readings of a diverse literary canon, personal and group reflections on the impact of race/ethnicity on identity development, and the composition of creative and critical writing responses in the course afford students and teacher alike an opportunity to work toward personal growth and communal flourishing. The seminar design exemplifies precisely the ethical pedagogy required of the modern educator to promote and account for social progress, the sort of progress that lifts up those often underserved members of our community.

The learning in this unit should not be easy. Conflict should not be evaded for the sake of comfort or a concern for the fragility of the privileged. Vulnerability is a necessary prerequisite by all parties if students and teachers hope to reach the level of growth the conversations, activities, and assessment prescribe. Be intentional in the approach, trusting in the unit as planned. Be assured that students will improve their writing and critical thinking skills. They will develop a clearer understanding of who they are, developing a deeper pride in that identity. Students will grow together in community. It's only English class, yes, but these small steps toward a common flourishing are real and necessary for enhanced self and social awareness.

INTERLUDE BY JANE BLEASDALE

This chapter is personally exciting for me as the editor because I have journeyed with Austin Pidgeon through the process of making his classroom an inclusive space. English literature is the bastion of tradition and has often ignored alternative voices. Shakespeare is revered over August Wilson or Chaucer over Toni Morrison. In this chapter, Austin shares what he has accomplished in a real-life classroom situation over the past two to three years. He has boldly used his own privilege as a cis-gendered, white heterosexual male to challenge the *status quo* in his school. His challenge embodies an authentic commitment to ethical teaching toward the common good.

In Chapter 6, Alex Porter Macmillan lays out an instructional model of a course grounded in tradition becoming the host for a symposium of dialogue partners. The Roman Catholic commitment to the social praxis seeking the common good breaks open an inclusive space wherein the dignity of each participant is affirmed.

REFERENCES

1. Angelou, Maya. *Human Family*. https://allpoetry.com/Human-Family accessed 2019.
2. Hughes, Langston. *Theme for English* B. https://www.poetryfoundation.org/poems/47880/theme-for-english-b accessed 2019.
3. Shakira Garcia, Leslie. (2016). Growing Up First Generation American: The: In-between Identity." *The Odessey*. https://www.theodysseyonline.com/first-generation-american

Chapter 6

Ethical Decision-Making from the Roman Catholic Tradition

Alex Porter Macmillan

This chapter explores some of the ways in which the contemporary tradition of Roman Catholic ethics is a valuable resource for teachers at a public or independent school. There will be no dogmatism or prescriptive lessons about faith. The lessons assume that students have no knowledge about Catholicism and allow teachers to make use of the Roman Catholic tradition as one voice in a discussion of ethics. The vision of these lessons is to see the Catholic faith as a dialogue partner with students of all faiths or no faith at all.

UNIT DESCRIPTION: RESOURCES FOR ETHICAL DECISION-MAKING FROM THE ROMAN CATHOLIC TRADITION

The best word to describe how this chapter approaches religion is as "resource." Given that twenty-first-century adolescent spirituality generally rejects authority and any attempts to speak from a place from authority, it is assumed that the ethical tradition of the Catholic Church will thrive when it can be seen as beneficial to an individual's particular point of view. (Pew Research Center's 2014 *Religious Landscape Study* shows a 7 percent increase in religiously unaffiliated respondents from 2007 and 2014—a dramatic increase.)

For discussions of the secularization and changing views of religious authority, *see* Rossiter's (2018) *Life to the Full: The Changing Landscape of Contemporary Spirituality: Implications for Catholic School* and Smith's (2009) *Souls in Transition: The Religious and Spiritual Lives of Emerging Adults*.

The instructional praxis in this unit consists of six lesson plans.

Lesson 1: The Preferential Option for the Poor
Lesson 2: Social Ethics and Ecological Justice
Lesson 3: Reconciliation
Lesson 4: Conscience Formation
Lesson 5: Human Dignity
Lesson 6: Prophets and Contemporary Moral Exemplars

Lesson 1: The Preferential Option for the Poor

Topic: An ethics that prioritizes the vulnerable

Lesson Learning Outcomes
Students will

- articulate a definition of "preferential option for the poor."
- articulate a basic understanding of power and privilege.
- consider the moral obligation to put those without power first.
- apply the concept of preferential option for the poor to specific case studies.
- create unique moral dilemmas similar to their own life experience where the preferential option for the poor could be applied.

Activity:

I. Discussion and Definition

What is power? What is privilege? What do you think is meant by *the preferential option for the poor*?

Begin by having students write down their definitions of power and privilege and attempt to articulate what they think the preferential option for the poor means. Have students share their definitions. First, have students share in pair groups, then with the entire class. Write down definitions on the board to be referred to later. Use the following definitions where student understandings might fall short (alternatively, construct class definitions based on student answers).

Power—The ability of an individual or group to implement their desires or goals within a larger community.

Privilege—Unearned assets or advantages that enable a person to exert power in everyday life; areas where a person is not forced to confront their social identity or location compared to others in everyday situations (e.g. race, gender, or sexual orientation).

The Preferential Option for the Poor—As society is often judged by how it treats its most vulnerable members, the Roman Catholic tradition understands the preferential option for the poor as putting the needs of the poor and vulnerable before people with power or privilege. In other words, all other things being equal, marginalized groups are given priority over dominant groups wielding the systemic advantages granted to those with privilege. In theological terms, it is understood that God, as a God of grace and compassion, sides with and suffers with those who are marginalized by the dominant group.

II. Agree/Disagree Statements

Have students fill out the brief agree/disagree worksheet with the following:
Strongly Disagree   Disagree   Agree   Strongly Agree

1. It is easy for me to see how privilege functions in my community.
2. I am able to see areas of my life where I have privilege.
3. I can see how people with privilege are given many advantages.
4. I have observed how power is used (e.g., by a teacher) positively in my school.
5. I have observed how power is used (e.g., by a teacher) negatively in my school.
6. In our society, people with power are usually trusted more than people without power.
7. I am aware of concrete examples of how people with privilege and power navigate society more easily.
8. It is wrong to put powerful people first.

After students have completed the statements, have students discuss questions as they arise, with an emphasis on concrete ways in which they have seen power and privilege function in their own lives. This discussion should be a significant part of the day's activity.

Typically, this processing can take place with students sharing their responses in pairs and then having students volunteer to share their responses. The teacher should follow up on responses with an emphasis on challenging student responses.

The following are the typical questions that emerge from this kind of survey experience:

- How do I know I have privilege if I am unaware of it?
- I have a hard time in life, how is it I have power that others do not have?
- How is it fair to put people without power first?

It is important to respond to these kinds of questions in the moment and address them as best as possible; however, having students thinking through and sharing their own responses should be the mechanism through which students process the information.

III. Case Study

1. Have students review a case study and discuss in small groups.
2. Follow with a class-wide discussion. This discussion should emphasize power, privilege, and how the concept of the preferential option for the poor fits this context.

Sample Case:
Speech and Debate Club

You are in charge of selecting the officers for your school's Speech and Debate team, which will include a president, a vice president, a treasurer, and a secretary. These four officers will be responsible for all decision-making for the fifty-plus-person team and will make significant decisions regarding the team's direction. Historically, the officers have all been seniors who are graduating, but recently, this has led to a complete disregard for underclassmen, who are often not given the opportunity to compete at tournaments. You are lucky in that there have been a large number of applicants from a very qualified and diverse team.

Before looking at specific applicants, how will you determine who is considered qualified? How will you decide what makes a person qualified? How does a consideration of the preferential option for the poor come into play (or does it)? How will you prioritize the members of your team for these elite positions?

(Continued)

IV. Student-Written Case Studies

This exercise will hopefully be a transition between the social constructs of power, privilege, and the preferential option for the poor (discussed in light of responses to the survey and Debate Team case) and their experiences. Be sure to be in tune with the scenarios in which students encounter this in their own experience.

1. Students write their own case studies in response to the following prompt: "Write your own case study that presents a challenging dilemma in which the preferential option for the poor needs to be considered but does not automatically determine the outcome of the case. Utilize your own experience to form this case study, drawing on the concepts of power, privilege, and the preferential option for the poor. Based on what you have learned in class already, please draw upon the points from the discussion and what you have already experienced in class. Be prepared to share with the class."
2. Review several case studies and discuss with the class various scenarios as time allows. Again, aim to highlight where power, privilege and the preferential option for the poor fit each context. A second key is highlighting the ways in which these concepts are played out in students' everyday experiences.

How to write a case study

A case study is a situation or scenario with a short description that is designed to solicit a variety of views on a subject. The purpose of a case study is to create discussion that gives validity to different, often oppositional views (i.e. a case study might enable a valid perspective both in favor of and against whether war can ever have a just cause). A good case study will utilize the imagination of participants and encourage deeper questioning of the issue at hand.

When writing your own case study, you should be able to describe a few characteristics:

1) Describe each character in a sentence or two.
2) Describe the basic setting or context (explain the background to the situation that will set up the conflict or dilemma that is meant to highlight the issue.
3) Describe the dilemma or conflict in a way that gives validity to different perspectives on the issue.
4) Create discussion questions that will deepen the issue.

Forma

Note: For each assessment in the unit, students can create an *electronic portfolio* in which they keep their responses to track their own development. This can be done on a google drive or similar software, where both the instructor and the student peers can review.

Lesson 2: Social Ethics and Ecological Justice

Topic: Throwaway Culture, Throwaway People, Throwaway Earth
Pope Francis and the Connection between Social Ethics and Ecological Justice

Lesson Learning Outcomes
Students will

- articulate the role of the Pope in the Roman Catholic tradition in relationship to the moral teaching of the Catholic Church.
- describe Pope Francis's concept of *throwaway culture*.

- Synthesize Francis's concept of a *throwaway culture* with the dignity of the human person, ecological justice, and the preferential option for the poor.

I. Activity:

Activator: Have students write the word "Pope" in the middle of a sheet of paper. Have them create a mind map that connects any words they associate with the word.

Review the following: The Pope has a unique place in the Roman Catholic tradition in regard to the religion's understanding of *faith and morals*. Through official Church documents and its tradition, the Catholic Church views the Pope as the successor of *Peter*, a follower of Jesus. In 2018, this role was given to Pope Francis, who is the official teacher of the Catholic Church in all matters of faith and morals. In exploring the moral tradition of Roman Catholicism, the office of the Pope generally (and Pope Francis specifically) offers a tremendous amount of resources in understanding morality.

In 2015, Pope Francis wrote a *Papal Encyclical*, a letter to every person living on this planet. The letter carries special weight to members of the Catholic faith, and it also is meant to create dialogue between everyone on earth. The letter is titled *Laudato Si*, which means *Praise Be to You* (from the opening words of the letter). The letter's major theme is the caring for the environment and ecological justice as it relates to the impact of climate change on people, especially the poor.

II. Group work: Excerpts from *Laudato Si*

Groups select relevant passages (see excerpts here) for students to disseminate, responding to the following prompts:

1. Summarize the passage in a single sentence.
2. Explain how the passage discusses any of the following concepts: consumerism, preferential option for the poor, dignity of the human person, economic justice, throwaway culture, technology, and climate change.
3. How does the excerpt connect people, climate change, and consumerism? Limit responses (single sentence summaries) either digitally or together on a whiteboard/chalkboard.

III. Discussion: As a class, discuss the following questions:

1. What is the moral imperative being offered by the Pope?
2. What is *throwaway culture?* What do we throw away today? In the past twenty-four hours, what have you thrown away at home, at school, in the company of your friends, in your neighborhood?
3. How is the Pope connecting people, the environment, and the poor?

Promote additional questions as needed.

IV. Assessment: Students write a personal response to the following questions (roughly a page in length):

- What themes from Pope Francis's message speaks to me?
- Where do I see a throwaway culture in my own life and the lives of those around me?
- How do I see a connection between climate change, economics, and the poor?
- Who in your family, community, neighborhood, state, country, and religion has the role of moral teacher like Pope Francis does for Roman Catholics? What qualifies that person to have that responsibility?

As with the previous assessments, have students keep their responses together in an *electronic portfolio* that they will be able to review individually and with the instructor, if necessary.

Lesson 3: Reconciliation

Topic: Reconciliation in the Catholic tradition as a resource for justice and morality

Lesson Learning Outcomes
Students will

- describe the Catholic process of reconciliation.
- analyze and critically assess how reconciliation promotes the good life and compassion.
- critique common misunderstandings of reconciliation and forgiveness.
- apply the Catholic process of reconciliation to a particular historical example.

I. Activity:

Activator: Have students brainstorm in pairs or threes common conflicts that come up in teenage relationships. Encourage students to be as realistic as possible, enabling their common experiences of broken relationships. Emphasize experiences that they have seen in friends or personally experienced.

Collect some common scenarios described by students either on a whiteboard/chalkboard/digitally or the like. Keep them in a place that can be referenced later.

II. Lecture: Describe the basic components of the Catholic tradition of reconciliation.

The Catholic Church has Seven Sacraments, which are seven rituals or moments that the entire Roman Catholic Community privileges as common encounters with God.

One of the Seven Sacraments is called "The Sacrament of Reconciliation." In this sacrament, an individual seeks out forgiveness from a priest who represents Jesus and Jesus's community to the individual.

Reconciliation has the following three key components in the Catholic tradition:

 a. Contrition—the act of saying you are sorry. The first component of reconciliation is both the act of apologizing and the experience of remorse—that one recognizes internally that they have damaged a relationship that needs repair.
 b. Confession—naming the actual way in which you wronged someone. For this step, it is essential to define what was done wrong for the understanding of both parties (or the community).
 c. Penance—repairing the damage that was done. This component is what enables a relationship to be rebuilt and reconstructed. The person who caused damage in a relationship needs to work to rebuild the damage done that is both commensurate with the damage done and ongoing to demonstrate that the offense won't be repeated.

It is important to note that, in many examples of apologies, only the first two criteria are met. Without an accompanying action, the offended person has no reparation or assurance that the apology was real and the offender is kept from the experience of knowing they are forgiven or are able to work through their forgiveness.

 III. Student Stories of Broken Relationships

Have students return to relationships that they defined in the beginning of class. Have students outline for each of their defined relationships how each component of reconciliation could build more holistic relationships and contribute to the common good.

 IV. Small-Group Discussion: Reconciliation and the Common Good: Social Dimensions of Reconciliation

Share with students Pope John XXIII's definition of the Common Good, which he describes as *the sum total of conditions of social living, whereby persons are enabled more fully and readily to achieve their own perfection* (1961, *Mater et Magistra*). Ask students to imagine, if individual reconciliation can be seen through this lens, how reconciliation within a community might take place. Have students write down in groups the answers to the following questions:

- What is the difference between one individual harming another individual and communities harming one another? What does systemic injustice look like?
- How would reconciliation between communities be different than between individuals?
- What different steps or additional steps might be necessary to the healing of communities that have harmed one another?

After ten minutes, have students share their responses with the class.

V. A Catholic Perspective on Peacemaking

For peacemaking and restorative justice, the Catholic Church often utilizes a quote from the Book of Psalms (a set of Jewish poetry written before the Common Era). In chapter 85 of the book, it says (in reference to reconciling groups): "Love and truth will meet; justice and peace will kiss." The four criteria often used in a Catholic framework for peacemaking include: (1) Love (care or compassion for the other); (2) Truth (acknowledging the wrongs that have been done); (3) Justice (meeting the needs of those who have been marginalized); and (4) Peace (people are able to exist in a safe environment and live without fear). Describe these four elements to students and then *reflect back to them in their responses where they mentioned something similar to each of these.*

VI. Assessment

Students should research a particular example of a historical wrongdoing and the efforts for reconciliation or what the consequences of a lack of reconciliation have been. Students should be given a considerable amount of time and effort to explore particular social injustices. (Suggest that this activity be done first as a think/pair/share to think through a particular conflict; then students should spend time researching their own. Basic research skills and utilizing databases, libraries, and other on-campus resources will be critical to this component.)

- *Common examples may include (but are not limited to) the following:*
- Examples of European Colonialism
- Apartheid in South Africa
- Troubles in Northern Ireland
- Jim Crow Laws
- Slavery in the United States
- Japanese Internment Camps

Students should answer the following questions in their research:

1. Compile the basic events that occurred historically and why they are significant (two or three paragraphs). Utilizing research skills, be sure to evaluate and prioritize the central events that take place, explaining the cause and effect of each event.
2. Propose judgments regarding the injustices that have been committed, including who was responsible and who was harmed (two paragraphs).
3. Using each of the three criteria of reconciliation, describe how these have been completed or, if there is still a lack of completion, what issues may still linger as a result.

(Continued)

4. Explore the elements that may or may not exist described in Psalms for peacemaking. Explain the processes that are taking place (or are not taking place) for each of the four criteria.
5. Imagine and propose what still needs to be done for reconciliation in this social context or what ongoing penance continues to be done for the aggrieved group, including any hope moving forward.

The primary purpose of this assessment is for students to be able to apply both the individual criteria for reconciliation (that can be applied to a community) and the Catholic vision of peacemaking as described in Psalms 85. They should be able to build a familiarity with these concepts to apply them in their own lives and ethical frameworks. A secondary, but still important, purpose of this is for students to see the critical importance of reconciliation in a global perspective. That is, reconciliation and peacemaking aren't simply altruistic ideas for interpersonal relationships but are serious concepts that will help build an ethical world.

As with the previous assessments, have students keep their responses together in an electronic portfolio that they will be able to review individually and with the instructor, if necessary.

Lesson 4: Conscience Formation

Topic: Conscience Formation in the Social Media Age: What We Surround Ourselves with Matters and Determines How We See Right and Wrong

Lesson Learning Outcomes
Students will

- understand the Roman Catholic Church's definition of conscience.
- construct their own definition of conscience.
- explore how conscience is formed in the Roman Catholic Church's vision.
- explore how conscience is formed in the twenty-first century.
- examine their use of social media in relationship to conscience formation.

I. Activity:

Activator: Have students write down any words they associate with *conscience*. What does the word mean to them? (Hopefully, they will have a basic understanding of conscience as well as a variety of useful responses.)

Bring together student definitions/understandings of conscience. This can be achieved either by simply writing student responses on the board or by utilizing a digital bulletin board such as *Padlet* (see *padlet.com*). Be sure to write down key elements that come out of the discussion. (This can be brought together either by pairs or by small groups and then shared with the whole class or simply have students collect responses together on the board/using Google Docs or the like.)

Elements of conscience could include the following:

(1) a voice you hear in your interior self.
(2) the judgment by which you know right and wrong.
(3) the feeling you have when making a moral choice.

II. Lecture: The Catechism of the Catholic Church

For this lesson, it will be useful for students to understand the text known as *The Catechism of the Catholic Church*. Points should include:

Catechism of the Catholic Church is an official guidebook of teachings written by the leaders of the Catholic Church. Since the teachings of the Catholic Church are often written across several kinds of documents from a variety of sources, the Catechism was meant to be a collection of the essential teachings of the Church that would be easy to access. Much of the wisdom that has come from the Roman Catholic tradition is contained in the Catechism, and it is useful to find a basic understanding of the concepts in Catholic thought.

Criticisms of the Catechism have centered on the narrow view of the leadership of the Church (who are exclusively male and unmarried). Any reading must have this context in mind in understanding the point of the document, which is one of the central issues in approaching the Roman Catholic tradition.

Reading: *Catechism* Excerpts on *Conscience*

The Catechism offers insights into the concept of *conscience*. As they read, have students note the ways in which the Catechism's understanding of conscience is different from their own. Students utilize an online version of the Catechism (a public version is available at http://www.vatican.va/archive/ENG0015/_INDEX.HTM).

They may need some instruction on how to look up items in the Catechism. Recommended sections for student reading are as follows:

1776, 1777, 1778, 1783, 1784, and 1785.

The language herein may be challenging for students; it may be useful to refer them to a recent document from the U.S. Conference of Catholic Bishops (USCCB) writing for an audience that includes young adults. The USCCB (2015) specifically addresses the formation of conscience in *Forming Consciences for Faithful Citizenship: A Call to Political Responsibility from the Catholic Bishops of the United States with Introductory Note*, noting that the responsibility to form one's conscience rests with each individual.

They lay out that "conscience formation includes several elements. There is a desire to embrace goodness and truth. [T]his begins with a willingness and openness to seek the truth and what is right by studying relevant inspirational sources (for Catholics, this would include Scripture and Church teaching. For other religious traditions or no tradition at all, these sources can vary from relevant sacred texts to inspirational figures) so important to examine the facts and background information about various choices. Finally, prayerful reflection is essential to discern the will of God."

III. Discussion: Open up the class for discussion, with the following questions as prompts:

1. What is interesting or unusual about the Catholic Church's vision of conscience in these sections? How does one change their conscience, according to the view of the Church?
2. Key ideas which can be useful in understanding conscience:
    a. A person's conscience should always be followed, according to the Roman Catholic tradition. Note well: for a Church that emphasizes hierarchy, authority, and obedience, it is a critical point that one must always follow their conscience.
    b. The teachings (Scripture) of the Church can help to form one's conscience, but it should not replace one's conscience. In other words, outside sources are not to be followed blindly, but are meant to be transformative of a person's process.
    c. Immersion in Scripture is one of the tools that help form a person's conscience.
    d. Most importantly, students should be mindful of what they immerse themselves in.

(Continued)

IV. Assessment: Exploring Social Media and Conscience Formation

A person's conscience is formed by their environment; students should take time to explore the people who they surround themselves with and by whom they are regularly influenced.

Have students pick one social media platform (Twitter, Snapchat, etc.) and explore between five and ten people they actively follow/interact with. Have students write for each person they reflect on the following questions:

1. Name/handle of the person they follow/interact with on social media.
2. What type of person this is (e.g., friend, musician, politician)?
3. Look at three entries (i.e., tweets) that the person has written recently. Describe if they have a positive, neutral, or negative moral impact.
4. Write two or three sentences on how this individual creates a positive, neutral, or negative moral space for others to live in.
5. Applying the Catholic understanding of conscience, describe the ways in which the individual forms their conscience in relationship to this individual. Using specific language that you have learned from the Catholic tradition on conscience formation, to what degree does this person positively or negatively influence your conscience?

As with the previous assessments, have students keep their responses together in an electronic portfolio that they will be able to review individually and with the instructor, if necessary.

Lesson 5: Human Dignity

Topic: Human Dignity as Fundamental Principle of Ethical Decision-Making

Lesson Learning Outcomes
Students will

- identify and define the basic principles of Catholic Social Teaching.
- construct a definition of the life and dignity of the human person.
- propose ways in which human dignity is threatened.

I. Activity:

The Catholic vision of Social Teaching is centered around the dignity of the human person. This lesson attempts to have students create their own definition of dignity of the human person and describe ways in which that dignity is threatened.

Activator: First, ask students what the word *marginalization* means. Write *all* answers on the board. Be sure to circle answers that best represent the idea of marginalization. These could include the following:

- active repression of one's rights (freedom, dignity, etc.);
- a lack of freedom because of one's identity;
- an inability to have agency over one's own life;
- basic needs not being met;
- living in an unsafe environment.

It may be helpful to reference the United Nations Declaration of Human Rights, which includes the rights that should be afforded (https://www.un.org/en/universal-declaration-human-rights/).

After this has been defined, students should list groups in our society whom they feel have been/continue to be marginalized. Have students be concrete about populations who are pushed aside in our society. Examples could include but are in no way limited to people of color, migrants, homeless people, people with disabilities, LGBTQ+ people, women, elderly people, people of different faiths (e.g., Muslims, Jews), and the like.

I. Once students have created this list, have them try to articulate what specific needs or rights are being denied from these populations.

A simple example might be folks who are homeless, who, by definition, do not have adequate housing/shelter but also often lack other basic needs.

A more complex example might be people of color who face discrimination in a myriad of ways, including: microaggressions, unconscious bias, employment discrimination, racial profiling, a systemically racist criminal justice system, and the like.

The hope is for students to see that people can be marginalized in a variety of ways and that all of these rights and needs, which are denied to certain folks, are considered a denial of their *dignity*.

II. Group Discussion: Dignity

Share with students the following quote from Pope Francis:

How can it be that it is not a news item when an elderly homeless person dies of exposure, but it is when the stock market loses two points? This is a case of exclusion. Can we continue to stand by when food is thrown away while people are starving? This is a case of inequality. Today everything comes under the laws of competition and the survival of the fittest, where the powerful feed upon the powerless. As a result, a critical mass of people find themselves excluded and marginalized: without possibilities, without any means of escape. Human beings are themselves considered goods to be used and then discarded. We have created a *throw away* culture. It is no longer simply about exploitation and oppression, but something new.

Exclusion has to do with what it means to be a part of the society in which we live; those excluded are no longer society's underside or its fringes or its disenfranchised—they are no longer even a part of it. The excluded are not the *exploited* but the outcast, the *leftovers*. (Pope Francis, 2013, 153)

Have students discuss the following questions in groups of two or three:

1. What are key components of the Catholic vision of the dignity of the human person in these quotes?
2. Based on the earlier discussion on dignity, what is missing from these quotes? What would you want to add?
3. In response to these quotes and identifying the ways in which marginalized groups suffer from a *lack* of dignity, create a group definition of dignity of the human person that can be shared with the class.

   III. Collect responses and try to create a class definition of the *dignity of the human person* together.

Key elements might include the following:

- Basic needs are fulfilled (food, shelter, and water);
- Social needs are met (free to interact with others without any fear of discrimination);
- Different relationships are respected;
- People are prevented from fulfilling their own purpose or vision for life; and
- People are able to choose a faith (or lack thereof) and worship freely.

As a class, compare and contrast the definition of the dignity of the human person that students developed and the Catholic understanding of the dignity of the human person. Look for places of convergence and divergence to point out to students. Ask the class (class-wide discussion) why they agree or disagree with the Catholic vision of the dignity of the human person. Highlight for students how the Catholic definition of dignity of the human person and their own definitions tend to be more alike than different.

IV. Assessment: Personal Dignity Statement

Students should create a concise statement of how they want to commit themselves to the dignity of the human person in their own life.

Examples might include statements such as:

"I will commit myself to ensuring that every person, regardless of their race, is treated equally in my school, my city, and my country."

"I will uphold the dignity of people of every faith on earth and ensure the right to worship freely for all people."

The key should be including ways in which students will commit themselves to valuing the dignity of others. Students should recognize that human dignity is inherent to every person, and upholding that dignity takes work, particularly from those who do not face similar obstacles.

In addition to developing a statement of dignity for the human person, students should write down the places in which they are utilizing the Catholic tradition and the places in which they are writing down their definition, noting the commonalities between their vision and the Catholic vision.

As with the previous assessments, have students keep their responses together in an *electronic portfolio* that they will be able to review individually and with the instructor, if necessary.

Lesson 6: Prophets and Contemporary Moral Exemplars

Topic: Recognizing Those Who Do Good and Battle Evil

Lesson Learning Outcomes
Students will

1. identify and define moral role models in their lives.
2. identify and characterize the definition of a prophet in the Roman Catholic Tradition.
3. construct their own definition of a prophet.

I. Activity:

Activator: Have students write about someone they admire highlighting key traits they consider important about that person (two to three minutes). Have them consider: What makes a person morally admirable? Why do they like this person or find them to be a moral role model?

I. Discussion: Ask students to share the person they thought of and collect the key qualities they feel make people admirable. Qualities might include self-sacrificing, courageous, compassionate, loving, accepting, kind, generous, and so on.

- Follow this discussion by asking the following questions:
  o What is the purpose of a role model?
  o Why do we need role models in considering ethical issues and questions?
  o How do role models and leaders help us better understand ethical decision-making?

II. Lecture/Reading: Prophet

The Catholic tradition depends on the Jewish tradition for its definition of a prophet. For Catholics and Jews, the word *prophet* literally means *mouthpiece*. In other words, a prophet was designated by God to call communities away from wrongdoing.

This wrongdoing was often the mistreatment of the marginalized populations in society. Prophets tended to point out to those in power, typically kings, how they had mistreated the poor and vulnerable. Prophets revealed to society how those in power are doing wrong and can change their ways. Wrongdoing here can be seen as an individual act that damages others (e.g., if a king uses his power to have one of his subjects mistreated). In this case, a king would need to be *reformed*, that is, the wrongdoing pointed out and the subject's dignity be restored to whatever means possible. Injustice includes the systemic inequities that exist which facilitate and encourage wrongdoings to happen (e.g., asking why a king has the power to have one of his subjects to be mistreated would be a question of injustice). In this case, a king (and perhaps the entire system of a monarchy) would need to be *transformed*. A prophet denounces both the individual acts and the systemic issues that need to be addressed.

The Catholic tradition calls upon all adherents to be prophets—to call out the ways in which society is blind to its wrongdoing and become advocates for change. This responsibility falls to all people in various capacities.

III. Assessment: Research Paper

Students select a person whom they see as a prophet, one who calls out society for doing injustice. For this exercise, students should do research on someone in the broader culture about whom they know little but is a person that they admire. Students will need to spend some time exploring current models who are functioning as a prophet, and it is important that students choose someone relevant to *them*.

Instructors will need to have some openness to student responses, as relevancy to the student experience is key. While an instructor might find some of the students' choices questionable, they should be open and discerning toward student selections of who they consider *prophetic* as they examine various people acting in the world.

They should do the following:

1. Research key biographical details about this person, using reliable databases and research techniques.
2. Explain the major achievements of this person and why they are considered to be ethical. What makes them a prophet? What makes their behavior a moral example?
3. Examine the inspiration for this person—why did they decide to do what they did? Did they come from a specific moral or religious tradition that inspired their action?
4. Evaluate the legacy of this person. If they have died, how is their memory celebrated? If they have not died, what organizations or institutions exist to maintain the vision this person has? What social changes are these organizations or people related to them contributing to?
5. Reflect on the ways in which this person and their legacy is a prophet in the Catholic vision. In what ways do they represent the Catholic vision of a prophet? In what ways do they differ? How are their actions related to their spiritual convictions (or lack thereof)?

It is recommended that this be a three- or four-page research paper that explores each of these questions in some detail.

As with the previous assessments, have students keep their responses together in an electronic portfolio that they will be able to review individually and with the instructor, if necessary.

CONCLUSION

By exploring these six topics, students will have an appreciation for a specific religious tradition (Roman Catholicism) and its rich history and tradition of ethical thought. These six topics model how engagement in ethical dialogue serves the moral discernment of a person of any faith or no faith at all. By examining these specific topics, students consider the following:

(1) an ethical vision geared toward the most marginalized people in their communities;
(2) an application of principles that frame environmental ethics;
(3) the praxes of peacemaking and reconciliation in both individual and social lives;
(4) the tools to develop their own conscience in light of the culture in which they live;
(5) The moral necessity of human dignity in communal decision-making; and
(6) a vision of a moral exemplar and prophet whose characteristics call them toward the good.

The instructional models in this chapter open a space for students to try on the experience of moral decision-making grounded in the application of universal ethical principles from a particular religious tradition, encouraging students to live out those principles or seeking out comparable principles from other religious or philosophical communities.

INTERLUDE BY JANE BLEASDALE

To educators in the Roman Catholic community—we hope that you heard the deep passion and commitment that Alex Porter Macmillan lives every day as a teacher of religion in a Catholic school. To those from other traditions or teaching in public education, we hope you still read the chapter! There are resources and ideas that transcend one religious tradition. As an educator in a traditional school setting, Alex pushes the boundaries he works within—to challenge his students and colleagues to reflect on their beliefs and practices and to discern areas where they conflict with the common good.

His work is genuine, original, and engaging—and connects well with the next chapter on teaching U.S. history. For teachers of social studies, find in Tricia Land's instructional designs in Chapter 7 the interdisciplinary nature of U.S. history, turning the classroom into a culture of accountability and responsibility.

SUGGESTED READINGS

1. Pew Research Center. (2014). "Religious Landscape Study" in Religion and Public Life. accessed 2019. https://www.pewforum.org/religious-landscape-study/
2. Rossiter, Graham. (2018). Life to The Full The Changing Landscape of Catholic Spirituality: Implications for Catholic School Religious Education. Kensington, Australia: The Agora for Moral and Spiritual Education. https://www.ceist.ie/resource/life-to-the-full-the-changing-landscape-of-contemporary-spirituality/
3. Smith, Christian and Snell, Patricia. (2009). *Souls in Transition: The Religious and Spiritual Lives of Emerging Adults*. New York: Oxford University Press.
4. Pope Francis. (2013). *Evangelii Gaudium*. accessed June, 2019

Chapter 7

Critical Skills as the Foundations to Ethical U.S. History Lessons

Tricia Land

This chapter is intended to be used as an introductory unit to a U.S. history course that will provide teachers with the tools to strengthen learners' inquiry skills as a means to revealing bias and turning the classroom into a culture of accountability and responsibility in the pursuit of ethical U.S. history lessons.

UNIT DESCRIPTION

The all-too-common practices of teaching history with the use of one text or one voice is the greatest threat toward the ethical teaching of the subject. U.S. history teachers have a tremendous responsibility to introduce, expose, and model analysis of several perspectives and sources alongside their students with the use of various instructional and assessment strategies. This chapter, comprising eight lesson plans, will introduce several different approaches to engaging with historical content and critical historical skills to enhance U.S. history lessons for both educators and learners of history.

UNIT LEARNING OUTCOMES

Learners of history will develop various skills that will allow them to approach subsequent history lessons in an ethical and truthful way.

Introductory U.S. History Unit Outline

Lesson 1: Perspective and Author's Purpose
Lesson 2: What Is Truthful History?

Lesson 3: What Is Ethical History?
Lesson 4: Ethical Historical Interview
Lesson 5: Ethical Historical Debate
Lesson 6: Intersection with the Social Sciences
Lesson 7: Single Events versus Historical Trends
Lesson 8: Historical Inquiry Passion Project

CLASS NORMS AND DREAM TEAMS

When a course begins, the class community should establish norms so that the classroom climate allows learning to take place in a safe and meaningful way. Each class may establish and practice different norms, making each year a unique experience for both the learners and the teacher. Building upon established whole school core values leads to a higher possibility of transferring norms and values across the curriculum and within different settings at school.

One norm that is important to practice is *active listening*. Teachers support students in developing active listening skills by leading exercises that require them to listen closely and respond to or inquire about what they heard. These exercises can cultivate a classroom climate that is safe, where all participants feel valued and heard.

Dream teams are mentioned throughout this chapter in reference to groups that students are able to put together on their own. They then sit with those groups for a period of time. Once students feel more comfortable after establishing norms and active listening exercises, they create their dream teams.

When creating dream teams, students formulate three lists: two or three classmates they know well, two or three classmates they feel they would learn a lot from, and two or three classmates they want to get to know better. The teacher then goes through the dream team requests and creates teams that are as closely aligned to the student responses as possible. Dream teams can change monthly or quarterly as needed, though it is important to allow time for the teams to develop cooperation and trust.

ASSESSMENTS

The assessments for the following lessons are flexible depending on the learners' strengths, background knowledge, interests, and needs. Some lessons have assessment styles to consider, but in the end, each teacher will best know how to engage, challenge, and assess learners. Students use a *History Notebook* as a place to keep notes, thoughts, reflections, and other work throughout the year. This notebook can be used to assess student participation and engagement with the material.

Other assessment strategies addressing the lesson outcomes and essential questions or to further critical inquiry around a lesson include participation, written or verbal reflection, full group or small-group discussion, self-assessment, individual or group speeches, individual or group presentations, written essays, and more!

Lesson 1: Perspective and Author's Purpose

Topic: Recognizing Perspective and Authorial Purpose

Lesson Learning Outcomes
Students will

- identify the author's purpose in a selected text.
- identify the dynamics and complexities of leadership.
- detect perspectives that are missing from selected text.

Overview:
Students will be reading about John Chivington, a leader in two separate historical events in the United States. John Chivington was seen as a man who made successful tactical decisions to defeat the Confederate Army in the West and who prevented the South from establishing any significant posts in the West. Chivington was also a leader in the massacre of hundreds of Cheyenne and Arapaho men, women, and children just a few years after his successes with the Union Army. This controversial man, seen by many historians as someone who stood on the right side of history in one event but not in another, is an example of a figure who can be analyzed when students are learning about context, perspective, and leadership.

Prep Ahead of Time:
Teacher locates a passage beforehand about Chivington at Glorieta Pass beforehand.
Teacher locates a passage beforehand about Chivington at Sand Creek beforehand.
It is important to make necessary changes to the following readings ahead of time, depending on the needs and/or prior knowledge of your group of students. If your students need more context around the chosen events, you could add that information to the readings. If they already have enough understanding of the events, then you could add more detail or enhance the language of the readings. This lesson is unique in that there will be an element of shock in the activator that requires you to be discreet about gauging students' previous knowledge around these events for this specific lesson.
The readings should be formatted in the same way and should be about the same length so that students have the impression that they are all reading the same text. Discreetly distribute the different readings to different students, alternating rows or sections of your room.

Activator:
This lesson will be less powerful if you preview any of the day's activities with the students. Begin by just letting them know that you are assigning them an independent reading to be completed in the first eight to ten minutes of class. Every student will have the same amount of time to complete their assigned reading. If students finish early, see if they can begin to write down words they would use to describe Chivington. When the time is up, you will ask students to share aloud what they have written.

Central Activity/The Big Reveal!
Leadership is one of the most dynamic concepts to explore with students. Many *aha* moments as a teacher occur when students share findings from opposing texts. Once you see that students have finished up reading their separate readings—begin to have students share aloud adjectives or qualities of John Chivington and write them on the board for the class to see. Students can also walk up and independently write these qualities onto the board. There are minutes of shock and even outrage as one student calls out *hero* and another calls out *murderer*. Allow the class to sit in that opposition before revealing that they have read different passages. Students, believing they read the same text, will need to debrief with the teacher about how the readings are indeed about the same person but about two very different events and decision-making processes that the one person followed.

Wrap-Up/Discussion of Essential Questions:
Working off of the passion that the students displayed during the reveal, recenter them and see if the group can identify your purpose in this exercise. Allow time for students to speculate and you will hear them begin to bring up ideas of information, persuasion, perspective, and *more than one side to a story* type responses. This discussion can lead into rich discussion or writing exercises around the *essential questions*:

(1) Why is it critical to question and analyze sources of information?
(2) How does excluding perspective lead to unethical history lessons?
(3) What (±) impact can an author's motivation/perspective have on a historical text?
(4) Which perspectives are missing from these readings? How does that change your feelings about the text/author of the readings?
(5) Why would an author eliminate perspectives and voices from a selected text?
(6) What must always be considered when writing historical pieces?
(7) Is there a situation where it is ethical to alter or eliminate perspectives and voices from a selected text? Why or why not?

Assessment to Consider:
Students will locate a historical passage, a newspaper article (current or historic), or an entry in a U.S. history textbook. They will ask today's same essential questions to themselves after exploring and analyzing the passage they select. Students should complete the following questions for the assessment in their history notebook alongside their notes from the lesson itself.

1. What is the author's purpose in writing this passage?
2. Give three or four direct quotes from the passage to support your response to question 1.
3. Whose perspective (or which community/group's perspective) is not being considered by the author in the passage you found?
4. How does excluding perspectives lead to unethical history lessons?

Resources Needed:
Teacher locates a passage about Chivington at Glorieta Pass beforehand.
Teacher locates a passage about Chivington at Sand Creek beforehand.
History notebook.
Access to find a historical passage (textbook, web browser, newspaper database).

Lesson 2: What Is Truthful History?

Topic: What Makes a History Lesson Truthful?
(This topic may take more than one class period.)

Lesson Learning Outcomes
Students will

- individually define truth.
- create a class definition of truth through consensus-building.
- create a class list, through consensus-building, of the necessary components of a truthful history lesson.

Essential Questions:

- What are the components of a truthful history lesson?
- What impact can untrue history lessons have on the learner or a community of learners?

Activator:

Students will write down their individual definitions of *truth* as a *Do Now*. After giving students your regularly allotted time to write down their definition, have students then share their responses with their dream teams or groups that you have designated or randomized. Ask students to then create a group definition by consensus-building and combining frequently mentioned *pieces* of each individual definition.

Central Activity:

Have each group write their definition onto the board to show that they are finished. Once each group has written their definition, task the class with reworking the written definitions into one class definition, by consensus-building, that will be used to understand the meaning of the word *truth* and referred to throughout the unit—and even throughout the school year. It can be more effective and engaging to rework a definition with the students and model the circling of high frequency words to form a definition that includes input from each group's initial definition.

Now that there is a co-constructed definition of the word *truth*, begin to pose the essential questions to the class as the lesson's assessment. Discussion can be sparked by writing the questions onto the board and having students write their responses on the board, in their history notebooks, or by sharing thoughts aloud, and you can work as the notetaker.

Wrap-Up:

Revisit the class definition of *truth* and be sure that the students know that this definition will be used throughout the school year when considering truthful history lessons and source analysis.

Assessment to Consider:

In their history notebooks, have students independently reflect on and respond to the essential questions and the process of building a class definition of the word *truth*.

- Explain the purpose for building a common class definition of *truth*.
- What are the components of a truthful history lesson?
- What impact can untrue history lessons have on the learner or a community of learners?

Resources Needed:

- History notebook.

Lesson 3: What Is Ethical History?

Topic: What Makes a History Lesson Ethical?
(This topic may take more than one class period.)

Lesson Learning Outcomes
Students will

- individually define ethics.
- create a class definition of ethics through consensus-building.
- create a class list, through consensus-building, of the necessary components of an ethical history lesson.

Essential Questions:

- What are the components of an ethical history lesson?
- What is the relationship between truthful and ethical history lessons?
- Is it possible to be ethical and untruthful or truthful and immoral?

Activator:
Students will write down their individual definitions of *ethics/ethical* as a *Do Now*. After giving students the regularly allotted time to write down their definition, have students then share their responses with their dream teams or groups that you have designated or randomized. Ask students to then create a group definition by consensus-building and combining frequently mentioned *pieces* of each individual definition.

Central Activity:
Have each group write their definition onto the board to show that they are finished. Once each group has written their definition, task the class with reworking the written definitions into one class definition that will be used to understand the meaning of the word *ethical* and referred to throughout the unit—and even throughout the school year. I find it most effective and engaging to rework a definition with the students and model the circling of high frequency words to form a definition that includes input from each group's initial definition.
Now that there is a co-constructed definition of the word *ethical*, begin to pose the essential questions to the class. Discussion can be sparked by writing the questions onto the board and having students write their responses on the board, in their history notebooks, or by sharing thoughts aloud, and you can work as the notetaker.

Wrap-Up:
Revisit the class definition of *truth* and the definition of *ethical* and be sure that the students know that these definitions will be used throughout the school year when considering truthful and ethical approaches to learning history.

Assessment to Consider:
In their history notebooks, have students independently reflect on and respond to the essential questions and the process of building a class definition of the word *ethics*.

- Explain the purpose for building a common class definition of *ethics*.
- What are the components of an ethical history lesson?
- What is the relationship between truthful and ethical history lessons?
- Is it possible to be ethical and untruthful or truthful and immoral?

Resources Needed:

- History notebook.

Lesson 4: Ethical Historical Interview

Topic: Conducting an Ethical Historical Interview
(This topic may take two or three class periods.)

Lesson Learning Outcomes
Students will

- create a class list, through consensus-building, of the necessary components of an ethical historical interview.
- develop/practice interview skills.
- conduct an ethical interview with a person they know about a historical event that the interviewee has experienced.
- compare and contrast narrative from interview to primary and secondary sources about historical event.

Prep Ahead of Time:
Locate resources (e.g., lists, diagrams, videos, etc.) that include, describe, and/or demonstrate the necessary components of a personal/historical interview. *Brainpop.com* is a resource that has a "Conducting an Interview" video lesson that also links to primary sources around interviews and articles about conducting interviews. If your school site does not have access to *Brainpop.com*, there are countless "How to conduct an interview" videos available on YouTube. You can locate a few videos ahead of time to help students brainstorm their list of necessary components for a historical interview.

Class Period 1
Activator:
Brainstorm the components of an ethical interview with the class. What are the different parts of an interview? What would it look like when these components are carried out in an ethical way? What must happen or not happen in order to make the interview ethical and truthful (according to previously co-constructed class definition)? What is the impact that can be done when an interview is conducted in an unethical manner? Compare and contrast class list of interview components/interview ethics with lists from resources gathered ahead of time.

Central Activity:
Randomly arrange partner groups and have students prepare eight to ten practice interview questions that they will be asking their peer for the second half of the class period. Remind the students that they are to conduct the practice interview in a way that includes all listed necessary interview components and to focus specifically on conducting the interview in an ethical way (as defined by the group).
The list of necessary components may vary. Some critical components are to have students create questions ahead of time, research beforehand to strengthen background knowledge of the subject, written or audio recording of the interview with the interviewee's permission, active listening, gauging sensitive topics, and conducting the interview accordingly.

Wrap-Up:
Have students reflect independently or aloud on their/their partner's effectiveness in holding a practice interview. What will they do the same when completing the final interview? What will they do differently? Have students give constructive feedback to their partners. If you have not practiced feedback with the class, to encourage constructive and meaningful feedback, you can require students to use specific sentence starters.

Ideas for Constructive and Meaningful Feedback Sentence Starters:
I appreciate/admire the way you . . .
I noticed that you conducted the interview in an ethical way because you . . .
One important detail to remember is . . .

Class Period 2

Activator:
Task students with brainstorming historical events of interest that people they know have experienced firsthand or through the news by relation of place and time. You may want to engage students by sharing examples of events that you have experienced or can recall happening in your own lifetime.

Central Activity:
Students will generate eight to ten questions to ask about a historical event that someone they know has experienced. Remind the students that when they host their interviewee, in person or remotely, they are to include the interview components. It is also critical here to remind students of ways to navigate interviews in an ethical way. Have students discuss topics that may require extra sensitivity and awareness of the interviewee's verbal and nonverbal cues. With the class, put together a few strategies that students can use to redirect the interview if the dialogue becomes tense or emotional.

Post-Interview Reflection:
Students will self-reflect on their ability to conduct an interview in an ethical way as well as reflect on the content of the interview.

Suggested Questions for Student Self-Reflection:
In history notebooks, with partners, or aloud to the class, have students reflect on the following questions: What made your interview ethical? What made your interview truthful? How did our class definition of truthful and ethical history influence the way you conducted the interview? After conducting the interview, would you add any components to our necessary components list? What would you add? Which component is most important to holding a truthful/ethical interview? Explain your responses.

Suggested Questions for Interview Reflection:
To what extent is your interview story different or similar from the research you did about the historical event from other primary and secondary sources? Why is the interview content different or similar?

Assessment to Consider:
Students could be assessed on their final interview project in the areas of selecting a historical topic, forming questions, researching to align/compare interview with other primary and secondary sources, conducting the interview in an ethical way that includes all components, and self-reflection of their experience in conducting an ethical interview.

Homework: Outside of class time, learners will conduct an interview and complete interview self-reflection questions.

Resources Needed:
- Videos or articles that describe and/or demonstrate the necessary components of a personal/historical interview.
- Access to sources (https://www.archives.gov/education/research/primary-sources, https://www.docsteach.org/documents, course textbook, online news archives, etc.) about student selected historical events.
- History notebook.

Lesson 5: Ethical Historical Debate

Topic: The Art and Social Science of Ethical Historical Debate
(This lesson may take two to four class periods.)

The structure of Lesson 5 is similar to that of the structure of Lesson 4, Ethical Historical Interview as the class will create a list of necessary ethical debate components, students will analyze primary and secondary sources to strengthen background knowledge of the issues debated, and students will self-reflect on their ability to participate in an ethical debate while applying all necessary components in the process.

Lesson Learning Outcomes
Students will

- create a class list, through consensus-building, of the necessary components of an ethical historical debate.
- consider actors' perspectives and values when preparing for and participating in a class debate.
- analyze and cite primary sources when preparing for and participating in a class debate.

Prep Ahead of Time:
Locate resources that include, describe, and/or demonstrate the necessary components of a historical debate. Again, *Brainpop.com* has short but comprehensive videos and supplementary sources and articles around the skills and components of debate. If Brainpop.com is not accessible, there are several "How to" videos around debate frameworks and examples of the process on YouTube. The National Speech and Debate Association (https://www.speechanddebate.org) is a valuable resource to reference for debate frameworks, resources, rubrics, and the like.

Class Period 1
Activator:
Brainstorm the components of an ethical debate with the class. What are the different pieces of a debate? What would it look like when these components are carried out in an ethical way? What must happen or not happen in order to make the debate ethical and truthful (according to previously co-constructed class definitions)? What is the impact that can be done when a debate is conducted in an unethical manner? Compare class list of ethical debate components with lists from resources gathered ahead of time.

List of necessary components may vary depending on what the group comes up with. Some critical components include a debatable issue, opening statements, affirmative arguments (based on research), timed rounds for equal voice, opposition arguments (based on research), and closing statements.

Wrap-Up:
For a closing exercise, have students select a debatable topic and begin a list of both negative and affirmative arguments for their topic. Students can practice this skill independently or in pairs as they begin to develop an appreciation for the critical thinking and deliberation that is required when formulating arguments for a debate.

Class Periods 2–4

Subsequent debate classes can be structured in various ways depending on the amount of time that is available to spend on the preparation of research-based arguments and the skill of teams responding to the research that is used. Consider adjusting the amount of time that you give to each round in order to place more value on the development of impromptu speaking skills versus vast amounts of research gathering. When looking to develop impromptu speaking skills, several topics can be covered in one class period. If your learners would benefit more from the opportunity to prepare and research in depth around a topic, the process of preparing a one-topic debate could be spread out over several class days.

Debate Round Structure	Participant Structure Options
Affirmative Round	Individual
Negative Round	Small Group
Questioning/Preparation	Full Class
Affirmative Rebuttal	
Negative Rebuttal	

Suggested Roles in the Debate: Facilitator, affirmative individual or team, opposition individual or team, timekeeper, judges (watching for ethical debate components).

Assessment to Consider:

Use rubrics that exist already through the National Speech and Debate Association or debate and public speaking rubrics from http://rubistar.4teachers.org. Rubrics for various skills are available on Rubistar but can also be customized to fit the skills that you are focusing on within this lesson: research, collaborative work, public speaking, class debate, individual speech, impromptu speaking, and so on.

Resources Needed:
- Resources (suggested within lesson) that describe and/or demonstrate the necessary components of a historical debate.
- Access to primary and secondary sources to reference when participating in a class debate. (https://www.archives.gov/education/research/primary-sources, https://www.docsteach.org/documents, course textbook, online news archives, etc.)
- History notebook.

Lesson 6: Intersection with the Social Sciences

Topic: Intersection within the Social Sciences
(This lesson may take one or two class periods.)

Lesson Learning Outcomes

Students will

- define and distinguish differences between the social sciences.
- dissect a historical topic into the separate social sciences.
- analyze a historical topic through the lens of different social sciences.

Essential Question:

- To what extent has the intersection of geography, politics, and economics influenced and impacted historical decisions?

(Continued)

Prep Ahead of Time:
Dissect a historical decision/event into the separate social sciences (e.g., sociology, geography, politics, economics, history). Identify ways that each social science influenced or impacted the one historical decision/event—use your dissection as a model for the assessment/final goal of the lesson.

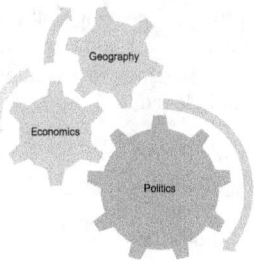

Activator:
The class will need to first break apart the definitions of each social science so that they are able to distinguish between each. The activator can be writing these terms on the board—sociology, geography, politics, economics, history—or having them on an activity page. Students should make word webs or concept maps with these terms at the center. This allows students to begin separating the terms and identifying ways in which they are frequently blended together in a history class but can also be analyzed as separate forces/pressures on historical decisions. Each student can create a concept map for each term or smalls groups can be assigned a term to diagram a concept map for each term and present to the class—depending on time and depth desired around definitions and understanding of these terms.

Central Activity:
After students have a strong concept of the differences between the social sciences, allow them to choose a historical event/decision they are interested in (event/decisions are used simultaneously here as many historical events occur because of decision-making). Students will then dissect the event/decision of their choice into a cog and wheel diagram that illustrates how each specific social science led to their event of choice.

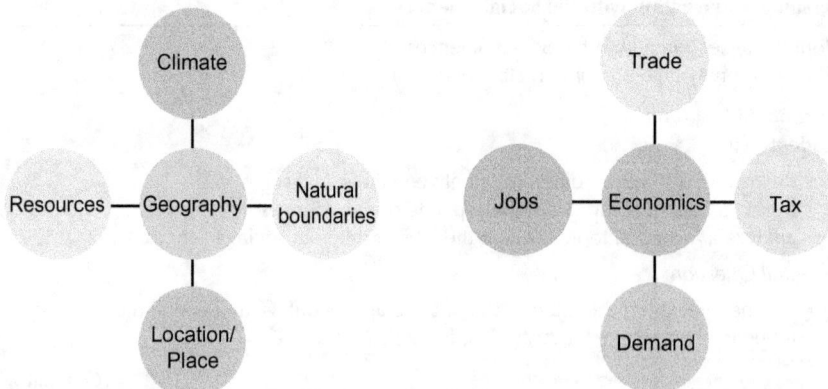

Wrap-Up:

As a wrap-up, students can present their concept maps or they could be displayed around the room for a gallery walk activity. The lessons could end in a discussion of the essential question or students could independently respond to the essential question for an exit ticket or homework in their history notebooks.

Assessment to Consider:

Creation of a concept map that separates the social sciences and their separate influences on an event.

Resources Needed:

- Access to sources (https://www.archives.gov/education/research/primary-sources, https://www.docsteach.org/documents, course textbook, online news archives, etc.) to support students in building a concept map around their selected event.
- History notebook.

Lesson 7: Single Events versus Historical Trends

Topic: Single Events versus Historical Trends

Lesson Learning Outcomes
Students will

- distinguish between a single issue and a historical trend.
- identify historical trends and root causes related to a single current issue by investigating the prevalence of the issue in reverse chronological order.

Overview:

This is a lesson with more magnitude than a traditional cause and effect skill-building exercise. Oftentimes, cause and effect activities involve single, linear graphic organizers that lack complexity, connection to larger historical patterns, and real-life meaning for students. Current issues and events are not isolated but instead require analysis of an entire arena of influence. Teachers must treat current issues as somewhat predictable results of generational influence and decision-making so that students can build plans of action to unite and respond to injustices. If learners are critical toward the information they receive from current event news sources and are able to recognize historical trends instead, it becomes possible to understand the impact that even seemingly small-scale decisions can have on a community long term. Tracing current issues back to their root causes from decades or generations ago will build the capacity for students to think critically around media discourse and the information they receive. If current issues are fueled by unethical decisions from positions of power but are understood more fully as students identify root causes to these issues, students can use their knowledge around historical patterns of influence to become agents of change for their communities.

Activator:

Begin class by inviting students to respond to this prompt on the dry erase board, a collaborative poster, or their individual history notebooks: *Name current issues in the United States that you know or think have been issues in this country for several generations.* Allow this activator to run for as long as students are adding to the issues list. The more issues that are added, the more clear the significance of this lesson will be.

(Continued)

Central Activity:

Students will select one current issue that they are interested in and they will begin looking back in time and researching related themes to identify early root causes and historical decisions that may have led to the cause of their event in current time. Students can create a reverse cause and effect concept map to organize their findings, possibly investigating prevalence of their selected issue within each decade, generation, or other measure of time.

Wrap-Up and Assessment to Consider:

Students will complete their reverse concept map and will independently journal (or share out to partners or to the whole class) about the greater historical trend that led to their current issue by reflecting on their historical findings. Consider requiring students to incorporate skills from Lesson 6 (Intersection with the Social Sciences) to explain which social, political, cultural, economic forces have led to their current event.

Resources Needed:

- Access to current event/issue sources.
- Access to sources (https://www.archives.gov/education/research/primary-sources, https://www.docsteach.org/documents, course textbook, online news archives, etc.) that support research on historical trends.
- History notebook.

Lesson 8: Historical Inquiry Passion Project

Topic: Passion Project: Culminating Inquiry Project
(This lesson may take four or five class periods.)

Lesson Learning Outcomes
Students will

- determine a question they have about any topic within the realm of the social sciences that they want to learn more about.
- research/analyze primary and secondary sources in order to fully answer their inquiry (i.e., identify context, historical significance/impact, intersection of different social sciences, etc.).
- apply skills and themes from throughout the unit to their research, presentation, and self-reflection.
- present their findings and takeaways to the class.

Overview:

The ethical teaching and learning of history is a never-ending praxis. Teachers and learners of history are accountable in the ongoing search for answers, the continuous pursuit of truth. The depth of knowledge when learning about a single historical day or figure can be as captivating as the study of entire ages or civilizations. All learners of history have unanswered questions and are rarely given the space or the tools to pursue or explore their questions, leaving them misinformed, underinformed, or uninterested in the subject entirely. Opportunities for Passion Projects are always overwhelmingly appreciated by learners as they actively choose their topics of study without the confinements of traditional or monotonous learning and instruction.

Encouraging learner's choice through passion projects is congruent with the ethical teaching of the subject as it breaks the restraints of traditional chronological curriculum and allows students to become active participants in their own learning while applying skills built throughout this teaching ethics history unit. The learner becomes responsible for seeking answers and pursuing truth around their long-standing historical curiosity or one that develops even after the introduction of this project.

The Passion Project should be presented not only as an opportunity to explore any historical curiosity but also as the culminating project to exemplify growth, acquisition, and application of the themes covered in this introductory U.S. history unit (i.e., truthful and ethical history, author's motive and perspective, analysis and inclusion of sources, consideration of the intersection of the social sciences, and greater impact of any [ethical/unethical] historical decision-making within their topic).[1]

Examples of Passion Project Questions of Interest Are as Follows:
What happened at the Boston Massacre?
Why did World War I start?
How have immigration laws changed in the United States over time?
Who was excluded from the writing of the Constitution?

Timeline to consider:
Class 1 Objective: Choose Historical Inquiry
Class 2–3 Objective: Research/Source Analysis
Class 4–5 Objective: Presentations of Findings and Audience Questions

Assessment to Consider:
Students will be assessed on their question of interest, research, source analysis, and presentation of findings. As this is the unit's cumulative project, students will also be assessed on the application of the unit's themes and skills to their Passion Project (truthful and ethical history, author's motive and perspective, analysis and inclusion of sources, consideration of the intersection of the social sciences, and greater impact of any [ethical/unethical] historical decision-making within their topic).

Resources Needed:
- Students will be gathering primary and secondary sources on their own, using the skills that they have built thus far regarding perspective and class definitions of ethical and truthful, to support their questions of interest.
- History notebook.
- Other necessary resources vary depending on the medium of the project. Students can choose to create a Google Slides presentation, video, podcast, interactive lesson with the class, poster display, and the like.

CONCLUSION

The beginning of this chapter warned that the traditional practice of teaching history with one text and one voice is the greatest threat against the ethical teaching of the subject. It is imperative, through community building and common language, to equip learners with the skills to recognize and challenge unethical analysis of information, the silencing of perspectives, and bias in historical thinking. The lessons that have been provided here have been designed and practiced in classrooms where norms have been established and where learners feel valued and responsible for navigating their own intellectual curiosities around historical happenings.

Only when a classroom community is continuously nourished can educators and learners experience an environment where all can hold each other responsible and accountable in the pursuit of ethical history lessons. With foundation and guidance, learners become conscious and eager to test their critical historical thinking skills not only in the classroom but also in recognizing and responding to current injustices.

INTERLUDE BY JANE BLEASDALE

Perspectives on the teaching of U.S. history, and most notably the resources used to teach, have gone as far as the Supreme Court for adjudication. Texts that tell U.S. history in a way that ignores much of what has really happened have been used for decades in our classrooms. In this chapter, Tricia Land calls us to engage the teaching and learning of history in an ethical way.

In the following chapter, Robert C. Bonfiglio sustains Tricia's commitment to transform classrooms into spaces for critical ethical and social awareness. Robert unsettles the student moral imagination and disturbs their passive expectations about learning Math by asking: *Whose truth matters?*

NOTE

1. Questions can appear simple but when learners are encouraged to apply the themes of the unit they will be required to go into depth with their research in order to align their findings with each crucial component listed earlier.

Chapter 8

Ethics in Mathematics Classroom Discussions

Robert C. Bonfiglio

Mathematics stands apart from other disciplines in its traditional emphasis on procedures and rules. This chapter focuses on incorporating mathematical concepts and methods into discussions on ethics, providing insight into questions like *Whose truth matters?* and *How does problem solving translate to considering ethical debates?* It also suggests that students examine their own place within mathematical learning and consider ethical concerns inherent in the field.

Traditional mathematics instruction has a tendency to divide classes into those students who love math and need little motivation and those who struggle and lose confidence. A lot of time can be spent preparing for standardized tests or practicing rote procedures. The idea that math teaches a *good* work ethic can be tiresome for students to hear when they are struggling with specific concepts. It becomes a cyclical argument: work harder to understand the material and understand the material to be a better worker.

The following lessons open up avenues for discussion in math classes and move away from the rigidity of practice and memorization. There is plenty of space for discussions on ethics and equity among all the computations and conceptual thinking.

It can be challenging to have ethics discussions when students have an expectation to approach their mathematical learning in ways different from their other subjects. There are structural choices, however, that make these conversations more accessible. Pencils should be used to encourage becoming comfortable making mistakes. Calculators' utility should be taught and their use restricted to specific situations. Word problems should reflect students and their own experiences. This choice presents a foundation for realizing that ethics "grows out of the real-life stories that people like you and I actually live, and love, and tell" (Nash, 2007: 1).

Teaching ethics in mathematics classrooms should go beyond showing *Hidden Figures*. There are creative opportunities to be taken. For example, developing through technological innovations comparative approaches to problem-solving in international classrooms. Such collaborations would necessitate cross-cultural discussions and an introduction to new perspectives and beliefs.

Even though sometimes math can be rigid, it is important to let students talk and share their experiences, even if this means taking a momentary break from computation and preparation for mandated tests. Mathematics learning must have a social purpose other than achieving a certain score. It is a field where individuals can be motivated to explore philosophical questions around human relationships, questions that lead to discussions on social justice, equality and equity, and duties of citizens and civilizations.

The following lessons provide opportunities for students to reflect on ethical issues and to consider why they are studying mathematics. Self-awareness about the subject can help lead them to think more critically, accept their own ignorance as an opportunity, be more open to other perspectives, and ask questions.

Some of these lessons will be specific to different courses, though there are components from each that can be applied across the discipline. There is an increased emphasis on relaxing a procedure-focused teaching approach to make space for student input that highlights their own experiences.

Unit Learning Outcomes:

- Students will examine their own motivations for learning mathematics and compare and contrast these to others' motivations.
- Students will approach mathematics as its own language, open to different interpretation and translation.
- Students will demonstrate probability and other statistical methods as a foundation for asking and discussing ethical questions.
- Students will use theorems as the basis for examining their own truths in relation to others' perceptions.
- Students will become comfortable leaving questions unanswered and understand the necessity for ongoing conversation in ethical concerns.
- Students will explore different motivations and paradigms for conducting research using statistics.
- Students will interrogate equity concerns in mathematician representation.

Lesson 1: Contextualizing Mathematical Learning

Topic: Exploring Individual and Class Motivations for Studying Mathematics

This lesson is in use at the start of the year for an elective course (precalculus), but it could be extended to any course.

Lesson Learning Outcomes
Students will

- verbalize their own motivations for being in this class.
- contextualize this (elective) class for their future learning (e.g., college goals).
- articulate and understand each other's anxiety around math.

The overall goal in this lesson is to lay the groundwork for making the classroom a comfortable place to make mistakes, something students are wary to do, especially in mathematics.

This lesson can be and should be revisited throughout the year to remind students of why they are taking the course.

Central Activity

- Instruct students to write independently on their own motivations for taking precalculus. (*Do I want to take calculus? Am I challenging myself? Do I think this course would not be a lot of work? Are my parents making me take this course?*)
- Welcome and encourage students to share with the class what they have written. Feel free to record visually on the board.
- Make clear that the course is an elective, and it is ultimately a choice that they have made to be here; each individual choice by every student might be different but each one is valid and should be supported by the class. Additionally, these motivations might change throughout the year, and some students might need guidance, from their peers, in making these changes. This is an example of providing an opportunity to address social-emotional learning, something sorely needed in the mathematics classroom. It is often a space of extra pressures to perform, insecurities around ability, and time constraints. Explicitly offering a moment of reflection helps to prepare students both to learn mathematical concepts and procedures and to contextualize their learning within their own and their classmates' values.

Wrap-Up: Math Anxiety

Show Orly Rubinsten's TED Talk *Why do people get so anxious about math?* The goal is to give math anxiety a name. It is a phenomenon many students and teachers deal with, and showing the video or discussing it upfront at least can help reassure students by putting *a name to the problem*.

Welcome comments and thoughts on the concept with the goal in mind of focusing on how math anxiety can contribute to students' motivations for taking this course.

Brainstorm together things the class can do to help each other stay focused on their motivations and lessen anxiety around math. For example, I borrowed an oil diffuser from a colleague to plug in on test days at the request of some students (who knows if diffusers actually help).

This video has some good statements on gender representation in math and can be used to lead discussions around that as well (see Lesson 8 for further context).

Show this video after the first assessment of the year when students usually start claiming they are not good at taking tests. It may be helpful to show it soon before the first assessment as well.

After working to have students examine their own tendencies for learning mathematics, there should be action taken to deal with those tendencies, including anxieties. A different approach to learning mathematics can help. Such an approach distinct from focus on procedures and rules is provided.

Lesson 2: The Mathematical Language

Topic: Thinking of Mathematics Explicitly as a Language

This lesson can be used for any course, though it is most relevant to those that are theorem heavy, like geometry or calculus. One of the most exciting things students comment on is how math seems like its own language. It helps students break down the divide between math and other school subjects

Lesson Learning Outcomes
Students will

- see math's relation to other subjects, specifically foreign language and English.
- gain a sense of mathematical literacy.
- understand others' struggles in learning a language that is not their first language.
- gain a glimpse into deaf communities.

For courses that heavily utilize mathematical symbols, taking a day away from mathematical instruction or practice in order to focus on mathematical literacy can save time in the long run and ensure a stronger foundation for actual computational work.

Central Activity

- Introduce or summarize mathematical symbols that the class has encountered or will encounter: Σ (summation), $\exists$ (there exists), ∞ (infinity), Δ (change), $f(x)$ (function of x), <=> (if and only if), – (subtraction), and so on. It can be difficult to work with a textbook when theorems are written like: "If $f(x)$ has degree of $n \in \mathbf{R}^+$, then f has ≥ 1 zeros $\in \mathbf{C}$" (so says the Fundamental Theorem of Algebra). It is important for students to gain the literacy to be able to read something like this and understand what it is saying. This can be very difficult, though, for those who have never worked with so many symbols at once, new or familiar. The symbols can be introduced or summarized in a visual table, on a worksheet, in lecture, or through other means.
- Invite students to suggest how they approach learning a language and any struggles they have had in doing so.
- Introduce the concept of a second language. This could be done by having assigned a reading or relating to a novel taught in your school's English department or a popular film. An engaging take on this idea invites an American Sign Language interpreter to class to introduce how deaf people communicate. For many students, this is a language they had have little interaction with. It can help breed discussion of further struggles, but also the importance, in learning a language.

Wrap-Up/Assessment

- Conclude by articulating that part of the goal here is to view math through a different lens, which could provide excitement or motivation to some students that can help develop patience for when they encounter difficult computations.

- Assign for homework students to reflect (through either writing or a follow-up classroom discussion) upon why it is important to be able to communicate with others across cultural or language barriers. Challenge them to locate instances in their own experiences or in the news or on social media: interpreters needed for refugees seeking asylum, scientists collaborating to prevent nuclear disaster at Chernobyl, and the like.
- Assess literacy either with or without context. This can be done by matching symbols with their definitions or by giving students statements that they have or have not yet seen and having them translate or interpret them.
  1. Example: The Fundamental Theorem of Algebra: "If $f(x)$ has degree of $n \in \mathbf{R}^+$, then f has ≥ 1 zeros $\in \mathbf{C}$."

Response: *If a function of x has a degree of n, where n is an element of the set of positive real numbers, then that function has at least one zero or root that is an element of the set of complex numbers.*

Having provided in the first two lessons a basis for having students consciously reflect on their own approach to mathematical learning in the context of the larger class, explicit focus on ethical concerns can begin to be addressed. The following two lessons are examples of how to locate these concerns within specific subjects at any grade level: probability and statistics.

Lesson 3: Introduction to Probability

Topic: Probability and Its Relevance

Probability can be a tricky and unintuitive topic. I have found that it helps to contextualize probability to help students approach the actual computational work with more confidence. I have taught this lesson at the middle school level for pre-algebra work.

Lesson Learning Outcomes
Students will
- identify representations of probability.
- determine the importance and relevance of probability.

Central Activity
- Give students a news article: For example, in 2018, *What are the odds of Trump surviving 2018 in office? An expert crunches the numbers* Siemroth (2018).
- Give them time to read it on their own and annotate it. Instruct them to look specifically for instances of what they think might represent probability.
- Gather their input on what they highlighted and pulled from the text. Follow up by opening up for discussion. Do the numbers make sense? For example, does it make sense that *Trump only has a 33.3 percent chance of making it to the end of his term in January 2021*? Or does it make sense that there is a *77 percent or less probability that Trump survives 2018 in office*? Do these two statements support each other?

(Continued)

- Because this allows for students to offer their own opinions and for others to hear how others think or feel, it is simple to work in a discussion about the importance of listening to these statements. Even if 77 percent is a relatively high probability, what does the other 23 percent represent? Does 23 percent seem like a lot in this context? Ask questions that allow students to consider why numbers are important in these contexts. Whose opinions do these numbers represent? How small does a percentage need to be in order to represent an opinion that is overlooked? How does overlooking this opinion locate specific people as small, or disproportionate, themselves? What ethical consequences does this reveal in politics?

Wrap-Up

- Invite students, either in class or as homework, to find other representations of probability in the news or elsewhere. You can use this to lead further discussions later on or to encourage students to engage with the material.

Lesson 4: Discussion on Statistic Measurements

Topic: Statistical Measurements and Their Relevance

Statistics may be the most evident mathematical material when considering building in ethics into a lesson. After or as students are working with basic concepts, like mean, median, and mode, this lesson helps contextualize data and can realistically be taught at any level.

Lesson Learning Outcomes
Students will

- explore different interpretations of data.
- interrogate the meaning of outliers and their significance.
- relate personal experiences to data.

Central Activity

- Present to students a set of data and have them calculate statistical measurements: mean, mode, median, range, quartiles, and so on.
- Review together any mistakes and solutions before moving on to interpret the data. For example, focus on data on school shootings in the United States from online resources. Tell the class what the data represent after they have done calculations; this allows for their own conjectures on what the data might represent.
- Welcome suggestions as to what the data represent: *What offers a "better" perspective—mean or median? Is this data surprising? What might be some reasons for these numbers?* These discussions often reveal individuals' views on what they think cultural norms are. This presents a valuable opportunity for the class to listen to each other and discover new perspectives.
- Focus specifically on outliers. Is there a data point that is significant, and why? This offers up many different possibilities without any real risk of a student feeling like their perspective is incorrect. For instance, the shooting in Columbine, Colorado, in 1999, was certainly an outlier when it happened. Is this shooting still significant as school shootings have become more prevalent in the United States?
- Small-group discussions can help in this next part to brainstorm ideas before sharing with the rest of the class. Direct students to discuss what *significant* really means, asking *significant to whom*? What experiences have the students had that would lead them to believe this data point is significant or not? What is it about these experiences that lend their beliefs credibility or that makes them socially just? What have they heard in the news, through popular culture, or on social media about this topic? Who is behind those sources? Should the variety of sources be expanded?

Wrap-Up
- For homework, request students return to class with a dataset they would find interesting to discuss. While some students may go home and count how many different kinds of cookies are in their pantry, others may go online and bring back statistics on more personal material, like health care. This presents an opportunity to discuss citing materials, the importance in knowing where data come from, and how this could provide an opportunity for misinterpretation of data.
- Bias can be and should be discussed in this or the previous lesson.

Side Note

Present news articles to go through together as a class without requiring they do any computational work. For example, students once claimed that most shooters are male because women are less likely to pull a trigger on a gun. This led to a discussion about gender roles and expectations and an opportunity for students to challenge each other and share different perspectives.

The following lesson considers the major defense in learning mathematics: it is worth learning because it is truth. The next exercise introduces students to the relationship between theorems and students' own truths and perceptions of others' truths.

Lesson 5: Truth Tables

Topic: Exploring the Concept of Truth—Theorems

Truth tables are a creative way for students to interpret mathematical meaning. Incorporate them when trying to solidify students' understanding of certain theorems in precalculus and calculus, but because they are logic heavy, they are applicable to any level of math.

Learning Outcomes
Students will

- examine the relationships between statements and their contrapositives, inverses, and converses.
- explore different meanings of truth in sharing and comprehending different perspectives and experiences as informed by individuals' linguistic and regional, among other, associations.

Central Activity

- Present a theorem. One of the most important theorems for calculus states that *if $f(x)$ is differentiable at $x = c$, then $f(x)$ is continuous at $x = c$.* This often begs the question, if a function is continuous, then is it differentiable?
- Introduce and define "inverse," "converse," and "contrapositive."
- Solicit a true statement from a student and relate the concepts to it. For example, a student might say, *If someone lives in Rochester, then that person shops at Wegmans.*
  1. Inverse: *If someone does not live in Rochester, then that person does not shop at Wegmans.*

(Continued)

2. Converse: *If someone shops at Wegmans, then that person lives in Rochester.*
3. Contrapositive: *If someone does not shop at Wegmans, then that person does not live in Rochester.*

Continue to solicit statements until students can establish the pattern (that if the statement is true, then only the contrapositive need necessarily be true also).

Relate this back to the theorem being discussed: the statement *if a function is continuous, then is it differentiable* is the converse, not the contrapositive. Therefore, it is not necessarily true.

Wrap-Up

- Reflect on the statements the students came up with to explore what *truth* means. For example, Wegmans is a not-so inexpensive, though extremely popular, grocery store that was founded in Rochester, New York. It is probably not an uncommon belief that if you live in Rochester, then you shop at Wegmans. However, not everyone can afford to shop there, even if they do live in Rochester. Challenging students in this way can lead to opportunities to think more critically and be wary of making generalizing statements.
- Discuss how math is often a constant representation of truth. Have students look for gaps in logic or assumptions they have made in the statements they came up with. Encourage students to seek in the news or social media for contradictions or overly broad statements that overlook someone else's truth. This could be assigned as an exercise for homework.

The following lesson uses a trigonometric application to provide insight into how to have meaningful conversation around ethical questions that either cannot be answered or continually need to be reexamined. The instructor highlights the importance of showcasing different approaches to solving problems.

Lesson 6: Leaving Problems Unanswered

Topic: The Problem-Solving Process

It can be difficult for students to become comfortable with leaving things unfinished, especially in mathematics. Working with trigonometric identities is ideal for this lesson, because there is rarely one suggested procedure for students to follow.

Lesson Learning Outcomes
Students will

- explore the value in leaving things unanswered, specifically related to social issues.
- recognize the value in creativity and different perspectives.

Central Activity

- Present a problem for students to work on. The problem should be one that the class will have skills to work on, though not complete.
- Allow time to work on the problem, whether independently or in groups. Guide the class step by step at an appropriate pace to allow for time to reflect on mistakes and work further. Figure 8.1 shows an example of a problem that involves trigonometric identities.

> **Solve for x: $3 - \tan^2(2x) = 2\cos(x)$**
>
> $$3 - \frac{\sin^2(2x)}{\cos^2(2x)} = 2\cos(x)$$
>
> $$3\cos^2(2x) - \sin^2(2x) = 2\cos(x)\cos^2(2x)$$
>
> $$3\left[2\cos^2(x) - 1\right]^2 - [2\sin(x)\cos(x)]^2 = 2\cos(x)\left[2\cos^2(x) - 1\right]$$
>
> $$3\left[4\cos^4(x) - 4\cos^2(x) + 1\right] - 4\sin^2(x)\cos^2(x) = 2\cos(x)\left[4\cos^4(x) - 4\cos^2(x) + 1\right]$$
>
> $$12\cos^4(x) - 12\cos^2(x) + 3 - 4\left[1 - \cos^2(x)\right]\cos^2(x) = 8\cos^5(x) - 8\cos^3(x) + 2\cos(x)$$
>
> $$12\cos^4(x) - 12\cos^2(x) + 3 - 4\cos^2(x) + 4\cos^4(x) + = 8\cos^5(x) - 8\cos^3(x) + 2\cos(x)$$
>
> $$8\cos^5(x) - 12\cos^4(x) - 4\cos^4(x) - 8\cos^3(x) + 12\cos^2(x) + 2\cos(x) + 4\cos^2(x) - 3 = 0$$
>
> $$8\cos^5(x) - 16\cos^4(x) - 8\cos^3(x) + 16\cos^2(x) + 2\cos(x) - 3 = 0$$

This is a sketch of some steps that can be taken. Students will come up with different approaches, and these should be contrasted and celebrated.

- At this point, this problem has reached a high level of difficulty (the solutions to this particular problem will involve irrational numbers), especially given all the work and thinking it will have taken for the class to get here. Allow students to complete conjectures on how to continue solving. For example, this trigonometric-heavy equation looks as if it is in polynomial form. Could the rational root test be applied?

Wrap-Up

- Conclude this problem by asking the class for what they found helpful in this lesson: *Is there a drawback in leaving it unanswered? How does this process make you rethink your approach to mathematical thinking?*
- Leave the students with an exercise to take home and revisit it during another class period. The goal of this exercise is to have students brainstorm questions or ideas regarding social or global problems that have no clear solution in sight. Get specific for them: *Can climate change be resolved? Should gender operate along a binary? Should Catholic women be allowed into the priesthood?* This exercise might require a prior discussion on these specific topics; the experiences of the students should be catered to in terms of finding a question or issue that they would be able to relate to.
- In the later discussion after this exercise, be prepared to relate back to the original lesson: *What was difficult about discussing an issue with not only differing viewpoints but also no clear-cut solution? Why is it still necessary to discuss these issues? Who is at stake when discussing these issues?*

The next lesson, while specific to statistics, is relevant to anyone working with numbers: numbers form the basis for daily measurements and suppositions. Teacher and students examine internal biases and paradigms behind these measurements in the context of conducting research.

Lesson 7: Statistics – Why Do Research?

Topic: Statistics as Research and Internal Bias

Statistics is all about the numbers. This lesson puts an emphasis for students on understanding the implications in where these numbers come from. Ideally, this lesson would be used at the start of any major research project students would undertake.

Lesson Learning Outcomes
Students will

- Distinguish between postpositivism and constructivism
- Develop critical questions to ask when beginning research
- Explore their own and others' inherent biases and understand its influence in research
- Review the concept of bias, and have the class brainstorm independently or in groups

Central Activity

1. Review the concept of bias, and have the class brainstorm independently or in groups
2. Solicit from the class their ideas on the importance of gathering statistics. In other words, *why do research?*
3. Acknowledge and then steer the discussion away from ideas focused on traditional science (like cancer research). Focus on behavioral science: *Why do certain people act differently?* or *Why are certain groups of people viewed the way they are?* Anything students come up with about wanting to understand relationships between individuals or groups should be highlighted in this lesson.
4. Decide on a question students are interested in that has implications for certain individuals or groups within society. For example, *Why are there few hockey players who are black?* If desired, it would be fairly easy to pull the numbers and present to the class the numbers on players' race in the National Hockey League.
5. Their own biases: *What do you know about hockey? What do you know about athletes? Do you have any thoughts or ideas about people who are black?*
6. Rather than have the students justify the numbers or the statement that supports that there are few hockey players who are black, have them focus on developing questions they would want to ask when conducting the research, questions like, *Do hockey players come from specific communities? What age do people start learning hockey? Is hockey an expensive sport?* Have students develop questions that will challenge each others' personal biases.
7. Conclude the lesson by differentiating between postpositivism and constructivism. Explain that researchers operate under a specific paradigm, or set of beliefs, and this set of beliefs often influences how individuals go about their research. Therefore, the choice of paradigm is fraught with bias. This is a good opportunity to revisit the concept of mathematical truth discussed in lesson five. Explain that no interpretation of data is wrong. It is more so that it might be poorly supported in that every research study conducted has flaws and critiques. Hypotheses are meant to be contradicted. Much of this could be communicated through a brief and introductory lesson or reading assignment on research methods, highlighting how research builds on itself and leaves space for further conversation.

8. Have the students toy with whether they would want to approach the research question *Why are there few hockey players who are black?* with a postpositivist paradigm, one that suggests there is one objective truth, or a constructivist paradigm, one that suggests there are different truths and different possible and acceptable interpretations. *How might specific biases relate to the choice to use either paradigm for a certain question?*

Wrap-Up
- Ask the students to return to a later class having determined a research question that reveals their own biases. Ask them to write about or prepare to discuss what the importance is in understanding one's own internal bias. Make sure that these biases need not be inherently bad: ignorance is a good thing. It leads to opportunities for learning and sharing experiences. A bias might be something like someone rooting for Xavier basketball because of a personal connection to a family pet bulldog.
- A further assessment could involve students bringing in a news article or post on social media that reveals the bias of the writer.
- An alternative approach to this lesson could involve supplying students with a specific research study, either quantitative or qualitative, and having them try to locate any bias involved. There should be careful attention paid to who the researcher is and who the researched is. If a student did pick a qualitative approach, make sure they examine the researcher might have avoided using numbers; follow up by having the student consider how numbers and statistics could have benefited the researcher (applying a mixed methods approach). Depending on how advanced your students are, introducing the transformative paradigm concerning research is an opportunity to highlight research with implicit social justice motives.
- Introduce an ethnography for students to examine over the course of a semester. Give them a source that explores the effort put into research and a concrete example of a researcher going into another groups' community. For example, present *Dude, You're a Fag: Masculinity and Sexuality in High School*, by C. J. Pascoe, because of its high school context. Be sure to provide assistance with occasional academic jargon.

The final lesson impresses on students the need for building community within a classroom. Students learn to locate their own mathematical learning within the larger framework of the discipline. In doing so, it provides a concrete example of how the class is implicated in systems that need to be reexamined and how the class is required to assess their values in relation to these systems.

Lesson 8: A Break from Computation: Equity and Ethics

Topic: Inequities in Mathematics

After a long unit or before an upcoming school break, it can be difficult to teach effectively. Use this lesson multiple times throughout the year to keep students engaged when they are not in the right mindset to tackle mathematical computations.

Lesson Learning Outcomes
Students will

- how mathematics as a discipline perpetuates inequities.
- mathematics' role in ethics.

Central Activity

- Either assign students to read before class or read in class together an article that discusses math and equity concerns. One such article is "A Sort of Everyday Struggle" (Natanson, 2017).
- Guide students through questions that relate specifically to equity concerns in mathematics. For example, examine the statement: *Current and former students and faculty—male and female—say the department's dearth of female faculty and graduate students creates a discouraging environment for women undergraduates; that women in the department are often told to take easier classes than their male peers; and that, in a department dominated by men, everyday faculty-to-student and peer-to-peer interactions leave women feeling conspicuous and uncomfortable.*
- Gather from the class what reasons might explain these statements.
- Continue on: *The Department is aware of its gender issues and is working to resolve them. In the past few years, the department has offered senior professorships to at least three women—none of whom accepted the offers—and has stepped up efforts to recruit female graduate students.*
- Ask the class, *Why might the women have rejected the offers?*
- At this point and throughout the process, be careful to gauge how the class is feeling. Some students are ready to discuss these issues. Some are not. Have a goal going into the discussion: For example, present the idea that if you do not see yourself in a specific role in society, what effect does this have? So, as this article articulates, *"The common metaphor for the lack of women in STEM fields is the 'leaky pipe,' which means that not only are women candidates being overlooked due to perhaps implicit bias considerations, but also women are dropping out of the pipeline for lack of encouragement or lack of opportunity," (Natanson, 2017).*

Wrap-Up

- Resolve the discussion when the students are ready to move on. Do not force the discussion on them. It might be helpful to revisit the topic at a later time.
- Students will struggle, even on the concept that if you do not see yourself in a specific role in society (like black children who grow up watching hockey largely populated by white men), it can be difficult to go against that grain.

- Do not give up. Math class is just as important a place to discuss ethical issues as other classes. Using the subject itself as an avenue to explain inequities is a simple way to introduce this ability to think critically. There will be resistance. Some students may insist that *math is the great equalizer. If people do not study math, it's because they do not want to.* Follow up by having them explore racism in pools in the United States. *Why was it a big deal when Simone Manuel became the first African American woman to win an Olympic gold medal in swimming?* This approach clicked for some of my students: a black woman, who had grown up seeing little black representation in swimming because of systemic and historical injustice, had to overcome extreme struggle to complete her accomplishment. They could articulate that she was not simply the first to do it because no one else wanted to.
- The more an instructor talks about ethics and math, creating a space for the discussion, the more the students will want to.

CONCLUSION

In working through these lessons, it is important to remind yourself to be patient. There may be a hesitation by fellow faculty members and students to deviate from traditional math instruction that focuses on computation and procedural learning. There is too much fun and creativity in math to excuse students from thinking how they do in other disciplines.

Students should be comfortable learning how their understanding of math relates to discussing solutions to ethical problems. The nature of mathematics as truth is an opportunity unique to mathematics that allows students to examine their own values. Such values have an important place when considering mathematical concepts. Students should also see these different perspectives as an avenue to examine equity concerns within the discipline.

REFERENCES

Nash, Robert. (2007). "Real World Ethics: A Holistic, Problem-Solving Framework," taken from: Robert J. Nash. (2002). *Spirituality, Ethics, Religion, and Teaching: A Professor's Journey.* (New York: Peter Lang) and Robert J. Nash (2002). *"Real World" Ethics: Frameworks for Educators and Human Service Professionals.* New York: Teachers College Press, Columbia University. https://kimberlymoynahan.com/wp-content/uploads/2012/03/popular-real-world-ethics.pdf

Natanson, Hannah. (2017). "A Sort of Everyday Struggle." October 20, 2017. https://www.thecrimson.com/article/2017/10/20/everyday-struggle-women-math/.

Siemroth, Christoph. (2018). "What Are the Odds of Trump Surviving 2018 in Office? An Expert Crunches the Numbers." January 18, 2018. https://theconversation.

com/what-are-the-odds-of-trump-surviving-2018-in-office-an-expert-crunches-the-numbers-90047.

Rubinsten, Orly. (2017). "Why Do People Get So Anxious about Math?" March 27, 2017. https://kimberlymoynahan.com/wp-content/uploads/2012/03/popular-real-world-ethics.pdf.

INTERLUDE BY JANE BLEASDALE

When we first met Robert, the book was almost done. Unfortunately we had not been able to connect with a math educator in our work. As a math teacher Robert pointed out the gap in our work, the absence of a witness from mathematics, and what a missed opportunity for students and educators. We are so grateful and excited that Robert joined our group and as our newest educator has a personal experience and investment in this work. Robert knows only too well the opportunity and importance of ethics being included in the math classroom as essential to the education of the whole child. This chapter is an exciting call for educators to respond to an increasing need for the promotion of the common good in our classrooms and hallways.

Robert's chapter is the final contribution from the traditional school framework and his disruption of student expectations on where learning ethics happens sets the readers' vision on learning beyond the traditional classroom—highlighted by Dr. Richard Marfuggi's health care workshops with students who bring global social, emotional, and moral experiences in Chapter 9.

Chapter 9

Health Care Ethics for Adolescents: Stirring Self and Social Awareness

Richard Marfuggi

The received wisdom that ethics is a discipline best undertaken at the undergraduate level and the tacit corollary that adolescents are unable to engage in meaningful dialogue on a subject that has little impact on their young lives no longer holds. What follows is a discussion of high school students' ethical evolution through an extracurricular educational conference on leadership in medicine. Though this instructional model concentrates on things medical, the suggestions are readily adaptable to fit a variety of nonmedical scenarios and disciplines.

THE NATIONAL STUDENT LEADERSHIP CONFERENCE: SECONDARY EDUCATION BEYOND THE CLASSROOM

Health is defined as the state of being whole; it is not, as many may believe, simply the absence of disease. This is a concept worthy of discussion with students whether they aspire to careers in health care or any other field.

With the advent of the discipline of medical humanities, health, as defined earlier, is described as resting on two great pillars: the *science of medicine* and the *art of caring*. Before discussing this construct, one must distinguish between curing and healing. Practitioners are not always able to cure, but they are always able to foster healing.

With this distinction in mind, one realizes that concentrating on one pillar alone is not enough. For example, concentration solely in the science and technology of medicine produces, usually, excellent technicians, while attention only to caring fosters empathy but is ineffective in addressing the clinical needs of patients. The combination, however, produces healers who strive to restore health even to those who may not be cured.

It must be emphasized that this is not an either/or proposition but rather a both/and pursuit.

The National Student Leadership Conference (NSLC), founded in 1989, is sponsored by the National Student Leadership Foundation, a 501(c)3 nonprofit, nonpartisan, education organization. The NSLC's stated goal is to provide students with the opportunity to experience life on a college campus; develop essential leadership skills; and explore a future career through exciting simulations, exclusive site visits, and interactive meetings with renowned leaders in their chosen field. Of the twenty-six career areas, medicine and health care is the largest.

For nearly twenty years, the author has served as Academic Director (AD) of the NSLC on medicine and health care directing the academic sessions that welcome some 8,000 students per year (grades nine to twelve) from all fifty states of the United States and seventy countries. Students enroll in a session at the site of their choice (American University, Georgia Institute of Technology, Harvard Medical School, Northwestern University, Vanderbilt University, Rice University, University of California at Berkeley, University of Miami, University of Washington, or University of California at Los Angeles).

Each session runs for nine days integrating ethics with academic, leadership, and social activities. In a few days, students experience ethics as both a theoretical and an applied discipline with value to them as individuals, family/community members, future health care practitioners, and world citizens.

ARRIVAL

For many students, an NSLC session is their first experience: away from home, on an airplane, on a college campus, and being surrounded by total strangers. Most assume they will be attending summer school or nerd camp. The arrival tension is palpable but quickly dissipates over the first several hours of interaction as students realize that they will be learning in a stimulating, safe, and enjoyable place.

The first Leadership Challenge (a name given to any activity designed to take students out of their comfort zone) is the assignment, at random, to a Teaching Assistant (TA) group. (This helps ensure diversity by integrating students with peers from a range of geographical regions and backgrounds.) Each group is composed of twelve to fifteen students headed by a TA; there are commonly ten to eighteen TA groups per session. Larger groups may also have an Associate Teaching Assistant assigned.

LEADERSHIP

On arrival, each student receives a leadership handbook. The leaders use the handbook for all sessions, regardless of program specialty, and covers topics designed to help each student become more self-aware while improving social and communication skills. The handbook includes chapters on the following topics:

- Personality matrix
- Personality, conflict, and introspection
- Conflict resolution
- New learning processes in communication
- Art of negotiation
- Effective decision-making
- Time and stress management
- Intrapersonal communication and defining leadership
- Public speaking

ACADEMICS

Unlike the leadership handbook, students receive a course materials binder, which is specific to each program. For medicine and health care, the binder serves as an overview of each session covering the following topics:

- The foundations of medicine
- Health care in a cross-cultural world
- Medical ethics
- Ethical simulations
- An introduction to clinical medicine, emergency medicine, and surgery
- The arts and medicine
- Medicine in the twenty-first century
- Biomedical debates of the twenty-first century
- Appendix 1: Glossary of medical terms
- Appendix 2: Live from the heart (a supplement to a video of a coronary artery bypass operation)

Notice the heavy emphasis on the humanities in general and ethics in particular. Presenting these topics along with clinical material helps students appreciate the interdependency of the one with the other.

One year, 1,590 students completed a survey at the outset and again at the conclusion of each medicine and health care session. The survey measured student attitudes regarding the best preparation for careers in medicine and health care and asked them to choose between a straight science and mathematics curriculum versus one that integrated the liberal arts (medical humanities, including ethics) with studies in science and mathematics. The results were statistically significant and reliable (Marfuggi 2003, 182–221). Following is the summary:

1. Prior to attending the conference, the students thought a heavy concentration in science and mathematics was better preparation for a career in medicine and health care than they did after attending the conference.
2. After attending the conference, the students thought that a liberal arts course of study (that includes all premedical course requirements) was a better preparation for a career in medicine and health care than they did before attending the conference.
3. Before attending the conference, students were more likely to take almost all science and mathematics courses than they were after attending the conference.
4. Attending the conference did not change the finding that students thought mostly science and mathematics with some liberal arts was the course they would most likely pursue.
5. After attending the conference, the students thought they were more likely to take half science and mathematics and half liberal arts classes than they did before attending.
6. After attending the conference, the students thought they were more likely to take mostly liberal arts courses along with the required science and mathematics courses in preparation for a career in medicine and health care than they did before attending.
7. After attending the conference, the students thought they were more likely to take almost all liberal arts courses along with the required science and mathematics courses in preparation for a career in medicine and health care than they did before attending.

STANDARDIZED TESTING

Well-intentioned legislation coupled with a curriculum emphasizing the importance of STEM disciplines has made standardized testing the primary means of assessing student progress and teacher proficiency. Complying with the drive to standardized testing, most early and much secondary education is binary in nature as this format lends itself to standardized assessment. The simplest examples are questions that are composed to elicit yes/no or true/false answers. Similarly, multiple-choice questions are formulated to elicit only one correct answer. Under this construct, educators are pejoratively referred to as teaching to the test.

That model tells students that there is only one correct answer to each question and, not surprisingly, students come to assume that there is only one correct answer to any question. Because it does not lend itself to binary analysis, ethics is ill suited to this pedagogy. The reason for this poor fit, simply stated, is ambiguity.

AMBIGUITY

Ambiguity, or inexactness, is exemplified in the dilemma. Students are initially at sea when asked to resolve a dilemma because ambiguity is not compatible with their binary universe. This seeming contradiction is at once challenging, confusing, upsetting, and frustrating for the students; they ask how they can possibly score 100 percent on the test if there is not an absolute answer to a given question. They do not yet understand that the test is the test of life and is not the same as the tests of academic assessment.

Students respond best to hands-on examples rather than theoretical lectures. Each of the techniques presented here models learning that looks more like what students call real life than a standardized test: a real-world example.

Topic
Dilemma—One excellent way to introduce ethics is to present a real-world example of a dilemma
Attending to ambiguity, harm, benefit, and bias.

Unit Learning Outcomes
Students will

- evaluate how *harm* and *benefit* constitutes a significant position in any discussion of ethics.
- consider the moral necessity to move out of their binary thinking mode to engage in meaningful dialogue.
- discover that applied ethics is concerned primarily with harm and strives to lead one to choices that prevent, reduce, or eliminate harm.
- discern that, in the choice between options that are *simultaneously* good and bad, one is unable to avoid harm no matter the choice.

(Continued)

Lesson Learning Outcomes
Students will

- discover that applied ethics is concerned primarily with harm and strives to lead one to choices that prevent, reduce, or eliminate harm.
- discern that, in the choice between options that are *simultaneously* good and bad, one is unable to avoid harm no matter the choice.

Activity
Ask students if they would invest in and/or use an invention.

> The invention is something almost everyone *in the world* would want.
> The invention benefits everyone who has or uses it.
> Its use creates *billions* of jobs worldwide.
> Its use raises the standard of living worldwide.
> There is a high return on investment.

After emphasizing the benefits of such an invention, ask for a show of hands for all who would invest in and/or use the invention. Encourage all to raise their hands.
Then tell the students that you have some additional information to relay.

> Sadly, nearly 1,300,000 people will die each year from the worldwide use of this invention.

Ask if anyone would change their mind based on the new information. Ask, why?
Restate all of the benefits.

1. Ask again if they are still opposed to the use of the invention.
2. Ask what number would be acceptable?
3. Ask how many agree with the statements made, for example, that they would not use this invention unless no one was killed.

Assessment
At this point, there is often a degree of tension and unease.
One might state: *I'm sure none of you who raised your hands will ever own or ride in a car, bus, and so forth again!*
Journal: Reflect back on this exercise. What are you feeling, given your choices? What do you discover about the consideration of harm and benefit when making decisions? What do you experience when making personal or social decisions in the midst of situations that become dilemmas (there are claims in conflict) and you encounter ambiguity? How might biases that you have complicate the decision-making?

WILL IT BE ON THE TEST?

While most students find the previous exercise interesting and amusing, many do not appreciate the importance and practical application of such study. When asked—will it be on the test?—it is good to emphasize that, in some form or another, ethics will appear on standardized tests such as the

ACT, SAT, MCAT, LSAT, and the like. In addition, ethical dilemma–type questions are frequently incorporated into oral presentations such as college interviews, job interviews, and the like. This information resonates with the students as many are thinking about life after high school graduation; they want to be prepared.

Standardized tests notwithstanding, point out that students will face ethical dilemmas throughout their lives and that it is not too early to begin preparing for those realities. Use examples such as end-of-life decisions, school/workplace dishonesty, plagiarism, and the like.

BIAS, COMMUNICATION SKILLS, AND PUBLIC SPEAKING

When asked, students will usually state that they are not biased. It is important to point out the following: (1) virtually everyone has some bias—usually as a consequence of birth, ethnic origin, religion, politics, and the like and (2) bias in itself is not necessarily a bad thing (though biases are a bad thing when they are grounded in inaccurate and dehumanizing knowledge). The key is for students to recognize that problems arise when one tries to impose one's biases on others, especially without considering the content and efficacy of a bias.

Working in both plenary and TA group sessions, students participate in personality matrix evaluation and dyadic encounter activities. They hear discussions of conflict resolution and the art of negotiation. These activities imbue each student with a better self-awareness which, in turn, help them understand other points of view.

Leaders point out that the study of moral philosophy, including ethics, also helps improve skills of problem analysis, argument formulation, and logical presentation—skills that are invaluable to get one's point across. Teachers and assistants emphasize that no matter how smart a student is or how valuable their position on a topic, it is essential to be able to communicate that position if they wish to be understood, to understand, or to contribute to personal or social advancement. Again, specific examples help.

Since many will be applying to college or will be seeking employment, the leadership team presents questions for them to work on that employ problem analysis, argument formation, and logical presentation. Some examples are as follows:

- Why do you want to study/work in this field?
- Why do you want to study/work at this particular institution/business?
- Why do you think you are a good fit?
- Why do you think this institution/business is a good fit for you?

Due to session time constraints, this activity follows a Socratic model between leaders and students but leaves little time for extensive dialogue. Students are encouraged to accept the challenge, work out their responses, and write them down. When students return, teachers ask them to participate in mock interviews answering some of the questions listed earlier. (Their reflections serve as resources.)

As student self-awareness improves, teachers and assistants encourage them to hone their communication skills and overcome fears of public speaking. This coupling of leadership activities with applied ethics discussions encourages students to venture beyond their zone of comfort—for example, the mock interviews and ensuing conversations frequently surface awareness of personal and social biases. It is essential to explain to students that some unease or discomfort is not only understandable but also a good sign as it indicates that they are pushing their boundaries; in this sense, discomfort signifies learning.

LEADERSHIP CHALLENGE

Since students prefer hands-on experiences to lectures, each session begins with a leadership challenge. For the medicine and health care students, this takes the form of allocating limited resources. The scenario is based both on recent history and on the current fear of an animal virus mutating and infecting humans.

Topic
The Leadership Challenge—Allocating Limited Resources

Unit Learning Outcomes
Students will

1. decide on the best utilization of our resources.
2. focus on the individual patient, and eliminate some variables.
3. propose arguments defending or eliminating each candidate, providing medical, social, and ethical justifications.
4. reflect on their rationale for their medical position surfacing personal or social biases at work in their decision-making.

Lesson Learning Outcomes
Students will

1. learn what constitutes the *validity* of an argument.
2. learn that they should analyze opinions, whether their own or another's, to determine if those opinions are well founded.
3. learn that a well-formed opinion requires analysis of facts that, in turn, are assembled along a reasoned pathway leading to that opinion.
4. learn that the communication of the opinion in a logical, coherent manner through dialogue, writing, and/or public speaking contributes to effective leadership.

Activity
The instructional team enlists and films a group of students in the following situation:

Moderator: Good evening, NSLC medicine and health care students. We welcome you here tonight and present you with your first Leadership Challenge. You are all members of the Utilization Committee at the NSLC Hospital.

A medical crisis is unfolding, and you must decide on the best utilization of our resources. This video presents the situation.

Hospital Director: The bird flu has mutated and now infects humans; the epidemic is here. With treatment (fluid resuscitation and respiratory support), there is a 96 percent survival rate. Without treatment, the survival rate is 7 percent. Six desperately ill patients are in the Emergency Room, but the hospital has only one available ventilator available. Who should receive treatment?

Here is a thumbnail description of each patient.

Patient 1 G. I. Joe; sixty-two years old; career military; decorated veteran of the Gulf War; currently working in homeland security.

Patient 2 Ado Annie; twenty-three years old; dropped out of high school; three children aged five years, two years, and eight months; three absent fathers; works minimum wage job; aspires to beauty school.

Patient 3 Maddie Graham; twenty-five years old; served twenty-seven months for drug possession; got GED in prison; started landscape business; employs at-risk youth.

Patient 4 Ali Baba; five years old; child of illegal aliens; born in the United States.

Patient 5 Shelley Cooper; fifty-three years old; prominent HIV researcher; working on promising vaccine.

Patient 6 Big Deal; forty-two years old; celebrity; rap star; offers $32 million in exchange for treatment.

To help the students focus on the individual patient, eliminate some variables:

- All patients arrived at the ER at the same time.
- All are equally ill.
- Untreated patients will likely die.
- The treated patient will survive, that is, there is no concern that the treatment won't work.

Review the candidates, and give each student one vote. Then ask for a show of hands to indicate their decisions.

Next ask for arguments defending or eliminating each candidate. Encourage students to think not only about why they *chose* a given candidate but also why they chose to *eliminate* the others.

Pause so that students through a reflective conversation (like a Socratic Circle) might identify and discuss the reasons for bias that surface.

Assessment (A timed Free-write: Giving Each Prompt Four Minutes.)
Journaling: Invite students to compose a reflective experience on what they feel as they make their decisions, what they discover about the impact of their decisions on others, what personal and social factors influenced their decisions, what factors made their decision valid, what factors made other students decisions valid, how would they describe the medical ethics (the key values) that inform their decision (what were their ultimate concerns), and if their decision changed during the process, what factors informed that change.

After the Leadership Challenge assessment, there breaks open the opportunity for students to understand that what they are expressing could be described by one or more ethical concepts such as merit, fairness, utility, reward, punishment, resource utilization, equity or inequity, and the like. During this activity, the AD explains that these motives require justification and that such support often comes from ethical theory.

The correlation between student decisions and dynamics in moral philosophy provides a real-world example, which leads to discussions of teleology, deontology, principalism, egalitarianism, utilitarianism, libertarianism, virtue ethics, justice, beneficence, nonmaleficence, autonomy, and the like. Rather than beginning with discussions of ethical theory, applied ethics helps students understand the relevance of ethics to their own lives.

A key requirement is imparting the notion of the validity of an argument. Students learn that they must analyze opinions, whether their own or another's, to determine if those opinions are well founded. Here the overlap with the leadership activities is important. Students learn that a well-formed opinion requires analysis of facts that, in turn, are assembled along a reasoned pathway leading to that opinion. The next element is communication of the opinion in a logical, coherent manner through dialogue, writing, and/or public speaking.

THE ARTS

NSLC students are surprised and encouraged by the inclusion of the visual and performing arts in their program. Medical schools, as well as other institutions, use the arts as a means to develop observation skills, foster empathy, improve communication, and encourage self-awareness. Observation, to borrow from Thoreau, requires one to not just look at something but rather to see what lies before them. Thus, students are invited to enter into the arts as moral narrative.

PAINTING

Topic
The Arts—Perspective, Bias, and Empathy

Unit Learning Outcomes
Students will

1. encounter the arts as a means to moral and social self-awareness.
2. develop observation skills.
3. enhance empathy through practice within the experience.

4. improve communication skills, being understood.
5. deepen self-awareness especially what informs social perspectives and bias—awareness of others.

Lesson Learning Outcomes
Student will

- think about how implicit bias about others impacts persons and societies.
- distinguish between perspective and bias.
- participate in civil discourse with others around challenging issues.
- practice showing empathy for peers.

Activity
Students view two paintings, with identical names, of similar composition, by two different artists, created twenty-five years apart (see figures 9.1 and 9.2).

Figure 9.1 *The Money Changer and His Wife*, Massys, 1514.

(Continued)

Figure 9.2 *The Money Changer and His Wife*, Reymerswaele, 1539.

A Guided Writing:
Invite students to describe what they see (students note differences of background and costume)
Then invite students to describe the couples. What is their story (each couple)? The distinctions between the two couples? (For example, they may observe that the couple in the Massys painting appear healthy, if not particularly happy. In addition, the wife gazes longingly at the coins, distracted from her open religious text.)
Invite students to hear each other's stories, then discuss what message about health, money, and religion the artist might be sending.

Assessment
Journal: Invite students to reflect on *what you learn about your perspective (what informs the way you see and the judgments/conclusions you develop), others' perspectives, and the painters' perspectives*. What personal and social biases do students discover informing their perspectives and how they impact the way they tell the couples' stories?

Yes, This Really Works

Drawing on nearly two decades of experience, former students and staff submitted anecdotal comments on the effects on their own lives after being introduced to medical humanities and medical ethics during their tenure at NSLC.

All of those who first experienced NSLC as students expressed similar sentiments: "This was my very first exposure to medical ethics as a high school student. The simulations made me think about the difficult decisions medical providers face. I had never thought about balancing obvious benefits with sometimes hidden risks."

Some cited specific activities with surprising clarity. This is what one medical student said of an experience some seven years ago: "I vividly remember everyone's reaction to the example of the number of automobile deaths per year and watching them struggle to answer: is it ethical to continue allowing people to use 1,000 pound death machines to get to work every day?"

The same medical student elaborated on the value of this exercise: "As a medical student, for every drug that I learn, I am tested on what setting is it appropriate to use the drug and what could potentially go wrong. The earlier aspiring health care workers start thinking about this dilemma, the better. Medicine isn't always black and white."

Not all responders went to medical school, yet the effect on lives remained constant. "When is it ethical and permissible to perform X? There will always be some level of risk and some level of benefit. When does benefit outweigh risk? I think that teaching ethics is key, no matter the career."

Repeatedly, the interdependence of leadership and ethics served as a basis for comment. From a master of public health in health care administration: "Many students that come to NSLC are brilliant and can nail any standardized test. However, this is not what Medicine is anymore. Medicine is focused on multi-disciplinary, value-based care with ethics at the core of decision-making. Administrators now focus on public health services. I plan on using the ethics I've learned first through NSLC and later through my degree studies to improve the quality and costs of healthcare delivery."

From a radiation oncology nurse: "The most important thing about NSLC wasn't the program topic itself, but the overall shaping of leaders."

Awareness of the other surfaces in many comments. "Ethics is about thinking what's best for someone else, aside from your own convictions. That takes education to be able to think that way, to understand that all people think differently and that's okay, but what matters is the best for an individual, or population."

An orthopedic resident echoed these sentiments and added specifics:

"In a world in which we share every single one of our thoughts on social media and often blur the line between reality and fiction, it is imperative that we introduce the concepts of ethics to learners at a young age. Addressing these concepts in high school helps build a foundation for students to compare differing opinions regarding standards of human behavior, promotes critical thinking, and develops moral decision making skills."

The teaching of ethics provides value in both career and life. Everyone has or will face ethical dilemmas. Developing a sense of self and a sense of one's place in community makes that task bearable though not ever easy. This skill stems from education in ethics that cannot start too soon. The following cites the application to a medical career but applies to all. The program emphasizes the three great principles of medical ethics: respect for persons, beneficence, and justice. It seems appropriate to end with a comment on social justice:

"Medical school applicants are screened heavily for character traits that reflect good judgement. NSLC does a great job showing how quickly a sense of community and responsibility can crumble when someone has too much power. This is something I have thought about often throughout my education and will be essential for me to keep in mind as I am given more responsibility."

During the high school educational process, the extracurricular experience, like NSLC, calls for a challenge to the perceived wisdom that the most effective learning moment for ethics is at the undergraduate level. Adolescents are ready to be mindful of themselves and the societies in which they live.

REFERENCES

Marfuggi, Richard A. *Healing America's Health Care Education System – An Early Intervention Program for Future Health Care Workers*, Drew University, 2003, pp. 182–221, Madison, NJ.

National Student Leadership Conference: Washington D.C., Link for Medical Programs https://www.nslcleaders.org/youth-leadership-programs/summer-medical-programs/access date 2019.

INTERLUDE BY JANE BLEASDALE

The final chapter is one that comes from a less traditional source—but is an exciting element of the sciences, the arts, and health care education. As you reflect on this unique leadership program led by Richard Marfuggi, consider the ways in which leadership, particularly in the sciences, can be developed within our students as a tool for ethics and the common good. Thinking about the three elements of science–leadership–ethics is an excellent opportunity to address students' understanding of the common good and assess their self and social awareness.

Epilogue
Dominic Scibilia, Series Editor

Social-emotional learning invites instructors and students into a space wherein they develop and deepen self and social awareness. Much in the spirit and with the intention of social-emotional learning, the contributors herein *Social Conscience and Moral Responsibility—Teaching the Common Good in Secondary Education* practice the collaborative creation of a space wherein instructional voices offer diverse models on learning ethics committed to *the common good*.

The pedagogical praxis is *student-centered*. The lens through which reflections on instructional and learning praxes occur is bifocal: *equity and inclusion*. From the first chapter, by Julie Sullivan (who breaks open a conversation on reflecting together on learning and writing across the curriculum), through the final chapter, by Richard Marfuggi (who writes on transcending a received skepticism regarding an adolescent's capacity for moral imagination and reasoning), contributors model instruction that creates a community inviting students to speak up while breaking out from the binds of social powers that privilege some and dismiss others.

Each chapter disturbs the readers' instructional conscience, initiating a reflection that asks how we create communities with the common goods of equity and inclusion. Welcoming the many to live as one—an essential instructional vision for the United States during the twenty-first century.

Editor and Author Biographies

Dr. Jane Bleasdale (edition editor) is an assistant professor at the University of San Francisco School of Education and chair of the Department of Leadership Studies.

Robert C. Bonfiglio is a middle- and high-school mathematics teacher at McQuaid Jesuit, in Rochester, New York. He graduated from Oberlin College with a BA in comparative American studies and mathematics. He is currently pursuing his MS in education policy at the Warner School of Education at the University of Rochester.

Nicole M. Cuadro is a distance learning program administrator and part-time faculty member at the University of San Francisco. Nicole is an EdD student in the Organizational Leadership program at the University of San Francisco's School of Education.

Nancy Johnson James, MFA, education specialist, is an artist and special education teacher in the San Francisco Bay Area. She is also a faculty member for Alameda County Office of Education Integrated Learning Specialist Program, which focuses on arts-based learning.

Tricia Land is a middle school social studies teacher in San Francisco, California. Tricia recently graduated from the University of San Francisco's School of Education with an MA in transformational school leadership.

Dr. Alex Porter Macmillan is the chair of the Religious Studies Department at a Catholic high school in San Francisco. Alex graduated from the

University of San Francisco's School of Education with an EdD in Catholic educational leadership

Dr. Richard Marfuggi, MD, FACS, LLC, DMH, is on faculty at the Caspersen School of Graduate Studies at Drew University and Vice President of the Medical History Society of New Jersey.

Margaret Peterson currently serves as the executive director of the California World Language Project at Stanford University, Graduate School of Education. Margaret is an EdD student in the Organizational Leadership program at the University of San Francisco's School of Education.

Austin Pidgeon currently serves as Dean Of Students at a Catholic Jesuit high school in Phoenix, Arizona. He recently graduated from the University of San Francisco's School of Education with an MA in Catholic educational leadership.

Dominic P. Scibilia holds a PhD in religious studies. He is a retired teacher in secondary education in social ethics and assistant professor in religious studies.

Dr. Julie A. Sullivan is an assistant professor of rhetoric and language at the University of San Francisco. Julie holds an MFA in Creative Writing and graduated from the University of San Francisco's School of Education with an EdD in international and multicultural education.

www.ingramcontent.com/pod-product-compliance
Lightning Source LLC
Chambersburg PA
CBHW051813230426
43672CB00012B/2721